Hg2 Rome

A Hedonist's guide to

Rome

Written and photographed by
Catherine McCormack

A Hedonist's guide to Rome

Managing director – Tremayne Carew Pole
Marketing director – Sara Townsend
Series editor – Catherine Blake
Design – Katy Platt
Maps – Amber Sheers
Typesetting – Dorchester Typesetting
Repro – PDQ Digital Media Solutions
Printers – Printed in Italy by Printer Trento srl
Publisher – Filmer Ltd

Email – info@hg2.com
Website – www.hg2.com

First Published in the United Kingdom in December 2006 by
Filmer Ltd
47 Filmer Road,
London SW6 7JJ

ISBN – 1-905428-04-9 / 978-1-905428-04-5

Hg2 Rome

CONTENTS

How to…

A Hedonist's guide to… is broken down into easy to use sections:
Sleep, Eat, Drink, Snack, Party, Culture, Shop, Play and Info. In each of
these sections you will find detailed reviews and photographs. At the
front of the book you will find an introduction to the city and an
overview map, followed by introductions to the four main areas and
more detailed maps. On each of these maps you will see the places
that we have reviewed, laid out by section, highlighted on the map with
a symbol and a number. To find out about a particular place simply turn
to the relevant section, where all entries are listed alphabetically.
Alternatively, browse through a specific section (e.g. Eat) until you find
a restaurant that you like the look of. Next to your choice will be a
small coloured dot – each colour refers to a particular area of the city.
Simply turn to the relevant map to discover the location.

Updates

Hg2 have developed a network of journalists in each city to review the
best hotels, restaurants, bars, clubs, etc., and to keep track of the latest
developments – new places open up all the time, while others simply
fade away or just go out of style. To access our free updates as well as
the content of each guide, simply log onto our website www.Hg2.com
and register. We welcome your help. If you have any comments or
recommendations, please feel free to email us at info@hg2.com.

Book your hotel on Hg2.com

We believe that the key to a great city break is choosing the right
hotel. Our unique site now enables you to browse through our selection of hotels, using the interactive maps to give you a good feel for

the area as well as the nearby restaurants, bars, sights, etc., before you book. Hg2 has formed partnerships with the hotels featured in our guide to bring them to readers at the lowest possible price. Our site now incorporates special offers from selected hotels, as well as a diary of interesting events taking place, 'Inspire Me'.

The concept

A Hedonist's guide to… is designed to appeal to a more urbane and stylish traveller. The kind of traveller who is interested in gourmet food, elegant hotels and seriously chic bars – the traveller who feels the need to explore, shop and pamper themselves away from the crowds.

Our aim is to give you an insider's knowledge of a city, to make you feel like a well-heeled, sophisticated local and to take you to the most fashionable places in town to rub shoulders with the local glitterati.

In today's world work rules our life, and weekends away are few and far between; when we do manage to get away we want to have as much fun and to relax as much as possible with the minimum amount of stress. This guide is all about maximizing time. There is a photograph of each place we feature, so before you go you know exactly what you are getting into; choose a restaurant or bar that suits you and your needs.

We pride ourselves on our independence and our integrity. We eat in all the restaurants, drink in all the bars and go wild in the nightclubs – all totally incognito. We charge no one for the privilege for appearing in the guide, and every place is reviewed and included at our discretion.

We feel cities are best enjoyed by soaking up the atmosphere: wander the streets, indulge in some retail therapy, re-energize yourself with a massage and then get ready to eat like a king and party hard on the local scene.

Rome

There will never be too few reasons to visit Rome, and rarely a good excuse not to return again and again. The city is looking good these days as the grime of decades of neglect has been wiped off, partly provoked by the 2000 Giubileo. Rome has spruced up and is becoming a viable modern destination, no longer frozen in time and celluloid dreams but with its very own cosmopolitan agenda.

As a city Rome is culturally overwhelming – a palimpsest of nearly 2,800 years of history which can be traced from its foundation by Romulus (according to the historian Livy), and thence the glory days of Republic and Empire, the early Christian and Renaissance periods and the hegemony of papal patronage and power, through to the neoclassical and aggressive Fascist eras, all through its architecture. Each epoch has left its own definition, creating a glorious mix that reflects the story of much of the western world. Yet still Roma transcends any pigeonhole definitions.

The city is no longer defined by its ancient ruins and dusty churches. There's a thriving contemporary scene comprising art, nightlife, innovative architecture and cuisine, and the contrast between the traditional and new has proved increasingly stimulating. Up-and-coming areas such as Ostiense and San Lorenzo have all the creative dynamism of Berlin, Manhattan's Lower East side or London's Hoxton, softened with Mediterranean balminess.

Of course today, as ever, Rome is frustratingly chaotic and seemingly lawless. Surprisingly, however, the Romani are slaves to rules, whether it be what time of day you're allowed to drink a cappuccino, or what you should be wearing that season (and even more surprisingly, a mindless respect for petty bureaucracy).

Getting around on foot or by taxi is most advisable. Rome's metro system is limited for obvious reasons of archaeological preservation. Although much of the centre is closed to traffic you'll be dodging unapologetic *motorini* (scooters). Spot a true Roman by his ability to cross five lanes of traffic without flinching while on the phone.

There are some unspoken rules you must abide by if you want to keep your cool in Rome. Bear these two in mind: always have a long lunch, and never feel guilty about slackening the pace on the sightseeing. Rome has a funny knack of showing you what it wants when it wants, and rarely disappoints.

More than any other Italian city, Rome has the power to enrapture those who set foot on her soil and is as intoxicating for the first-time visitor as the long-time inhabitant. Despite all the pitfalls, brashness and intolerable chaos, when the sun shines over the Palatine hill and your belly is full of *bucatini amatriciana*, the sense of something very special and eternal stings the senses. *Viva Roma*.

SNACK

9. Caffè Capitolino

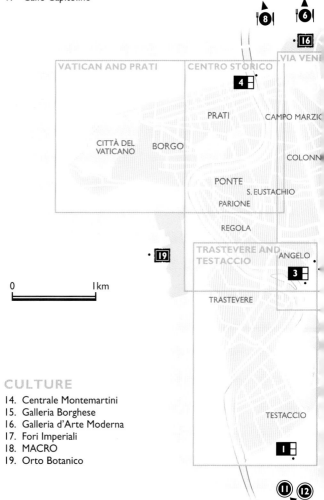

CULTURE

14. Centrale Montemartini
15. Galleria Borghese
16. Galleria d'Arte Moderna
17. Fori Imperiali
18. MACRO
19. Orto Botanico

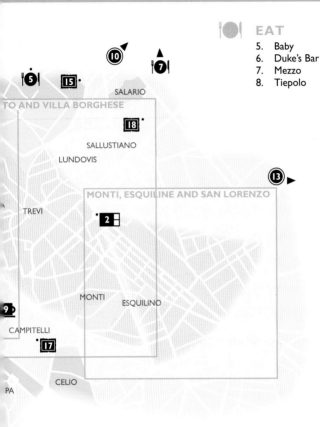

EAT

5. Baby
6. Duke's Bar
7. Mezzo
8. Tiepolo

SALARIO

TO AND VILLA BORGHESE

SALLUSTIANO

LUNDOVIS

MONTI, ESQUILINE AND SAN LORENZO

TREVI

MONTI

ESQUILINO

CAMPITELLI

CELIO

PA

SLEEP

1. Abitart
2. Exedra
3. Forty Seven
4. Locarno

PARTY

10. Brancaleone
11. Classico Village
12. Goa
13. La Palma

Centro Storico

Orientation in the Centro Storico is rather simple. The Via del Corso is the eponymous example of a Roman road which extends in a mile-long straight line from Piazza del Popolo in the north, to Piazza Venezia and the kitsch 'typewriter' Vittorio Emanuele monument (take one look and you'll understand the moniker). On one side are the Spanish Steps, Trevi fountain and Villa Borghese, while the other is a glorious labyrinth of streets towards the Pantheon and Piazza Navona and down towards the banks of the river and Castel Sant'Angelo.

Around the ruins of the Roman forum (behind the Vittorio Emanuele monument) is where the whole thing started, a piece of marshland which grew into a social and commercial centre and within the space of a few centuries ruled an empire which reached from Spain to Asia Minor.

Apart from sightseeing, shopping is the preferred pastime along the Via dei Condotti, Rome's answer to Bond Street. Connecting the Spanish Steps to Piazza del Popolo is the Via del Babuino, another designer shopping mecca and where you'll find cool concept store TAD, while Via del Governo Vecchio on the Centro Storico side is an essential bijou break from the crowds.

There are two places to buy icecream in the Centro Storico, San Crispino and Giolitti (see Snack). You won't eat bad icecream elsewhere, but stray from this advice to your palette's own loss.

For hassle-free high-speed cultural injections duck in and out of churches. They are often free galleries filled with masterpieces without the queues, crowds or tacky gift shops. Santa Maria del Popolo and San Luigi dei Francesi are easy vehicles to catch a few Caravaggio 'chiaroscuro' showstoppers.

The ebb and flow of tourist traffic and large, meandering groups from the Pantheon to the Spanish steps, along via del Corso to Piazza Navona, and the Trevi Fountain can be insanely infuriating, but unfortunately this is modern day Rome.

But for every rose-peddler that gets your goat there's an equal measure of things to make your heart melt, just as long as you make sure you duck into glamorous establishments for a restorative prosecco (perfectly acceptable anytime after midday), or a cool café (just remember the no cappuccino after 11am rule.)

Look for the refuges such as Via Margutta behind the Spanish Steps, or stop off under the fig tree at Bar del Fico and watch the weather-beaten veterans battle it out over an afternoon game of chess.

When it all gets too much with crowds, heat and Stendhal's syndrome (culture fatigue) it's normally time for aperitivo. The Romans would do exactly the same.

0   250m   500m

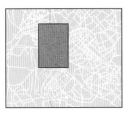

Via Veneto & Villa Borghese

The Via Veneto in its '50s and '60s glory days was once lined with cocktail palaces, Alfa Romeo sports cars and the glamorous traffic of starlets immortalized by Fellini in his film *La Dolce Vita*. These days it's the haunt of wide-eyed tourists buying T-shirts from the Hard Rock Café and looking for some bygone glitz over an *americano* cocktail. The high-octane nightlife may have waned but the ashes are still there in the Jackie O nightclub, an entertaining if a little staid glimpse into the history book of Roman nightclubbing. Whether related or not, most of the city's options for adult entertainment lurk in these parts, as well as a crop of the most luxuriant hotels such as the Eden, Aleph and the historic Rome Palace.

The strip extends north up to the leafy Villa Borghese, past the Piazza di Siena at the mouth of the park, with its random mix of showjumping arena, hot-air balloon and underground car park cum nightclub complex.

At the beginning of the 17th century it was the dream of the illustrious Cardinal Scipione Borghese to turn the family vineyards and surrounding lands into a baroque pleasure park, or a 'Theatre of the Universe', giving birth to the Villa Borghese, which is now a public park. Once intended as an impressive display for diplomats and heads of state, the Borghese, with its art galleries, aviary, exotic plants and curiosities, attracts less regal visitors these days – mostly tourists and families taking advantage of one of the few green lungs in the city centre. Although the grass is a little scrubby (there's better park life to be had at the Villa Doria Pamphili on the Janiculum hill) bike rides are a popular weekend activity and the views from the Pincio hill over the city's rooftops are exhilarating.

Ambassadorial villas still lurk behind the trees of the Galleria Nazionale d'Arte Moderna and there's a palpable sense of quiet refinement at the Michelin-starred restaurant Baby in the grounds of the Aldovrandi Palace hotel.

Northern Rome is becoming increasingly more fashionable with the city's young guns, although the bad transport links make it a little dislocated for visitors to explore with ease.

Trendy restaurants Mezzo, Tiepolo and Duke's Bar all lie north of the city's gate behind the Piazza del Popolo, along with the Stadium and the Auditorium. This is also where MAXXI, Rome's work-in-progress museum of contemporary art, is situated. The Via Salaria was an ancient salt trail which even pre-exists Rome itself, but is now a residential district surrounded by embassies and the leafy public gardens of Villa Ada. More contemporary art can be found around the Via Nomentana at the MACRO art gallery, which occupies the old Peroni beer factory.

DRINK

22. 7th Heaven Bar
23. Al Vino Al Vino
24. H Club Doney
25. Ice Club
26. La Terrazza
    Bar at the Hotel Eden
27. Stravinskij Bar

 EAT

18. F.I.S.H.
19. Il Margutta Ristorante
20. Palatium
21. La Terazza

 SLEEP

1. Aleph
2. Casa Howard
3. Capo d'Africa
4. Daphne Inn
5. Eden
6. Exedra
7. Hassler Roma
8. Hotel Art
9. Hotel de Russie
10. Inn at Forum
11. Inn at Spanish Steps
12. In Town
13. Il Palazzetto International Wine Academy
14. Portrait Suites
15. Rome Palace
16. St. Regis Grand
17. View at the Spanish Steps

```
0                 500m              1km
```

SHOP

- Via Babuino
- Via Borgognona
- Via Condotti
- Via del Corso
- Via Frattina

SNACK

28. Babington's
29. La Bottega del Caffè
30. Gelateria di San Crispino
31. Gina
32. L'Impiccione Viaggiatore
33. Palazzetto International Wine Academy
34. Tad Café
35. Thè Verde

CULTURE

40. San Clemente
41. Capitoline Museums
42. Colosseum
43. Keats/Shelley House
44. Palazzo Barberini
45. Santa Maria della Vittoria
46. Santa Maria Maggiore
47. Trevi Fountain

PARTY

36. Art Cafè
37. Gilda
38. Jackie-O
39. L'Oppio

Vatican and Prati

The Vatican is the smallest country in the world, occupying less than half a square kilometre and with only around 800 residents. It is, however, home to some of the greatest cultural treasures in the world, as well as being the headquarters of the Roman Catholic Church. It has its own diplomatic service, army (Swiss Guard), heliport, radio and TV stations and currency (Vatican euros have a minimal circulation). Many Romans will post their letters from the Vatican since its own postal service is infinitely more reliable than the national snail mail. Reportedly, it has better-stocked pharmacies too, and tax-free electrical goods.

When he's in Rome the Pope makes appearances at noon on Sundays from the window of his study, and addresses the crowd of pilgrims who gather in St Peter's Square. On Wednesdays he holds a general audience in the square, weather permitting.

Prati, the neighbourhood surrounding the Vatican, is civilized, residential and painfully bourgeois. For this reason nothing very exciting happens here. It's filled with eerily calm tree-lined boulevards and *grandes dames* in linen suits with coiffed hair riding bicycles, while the patter of pampered pooches is never far away. Cafés and bars house hordes of Pariolini (the term used to describe elegant Romans

from the Parioli district) nibbling on pastries and imbibing *prosecco* dressed in fur coats, with shiny cars parked outside.

The area started life as the meadows around the Renaissance ramparts to the Vatican, which were shorn up to make way for housing for the employees of the new ministries and parliament after Rome became the capital of unified Italy in 1871. It has been tenaciously 'white collar' ever since.

Although lacking the youthful vibrancy and colour you'll find in other parts of Rome, Prati has some very pleasant dining choices, including one of the city's most acclaimed restaurants, L'Arcangelo. The palm-lined Piazza Cavour is home to the Costantini *enoteca*, a decadent, old-fashioned wine bar and restaurant with heavy velvet drapes and dusty bottles on Art Deco shelves. The lunch spots Pupina and Del Frate are perfect for post-sightseeing sustenance at the Vatican.

The relaxed shopping promenade of Via Cola di Rienzo offers visitors the chance to indulge in a little retail therapy. In keeping with the style of the residents there's nothing wildly exciting here, but it's good for quality essentials and gifts (especially of the gourmet variety, at deli-catessens Castroni and Franchi).

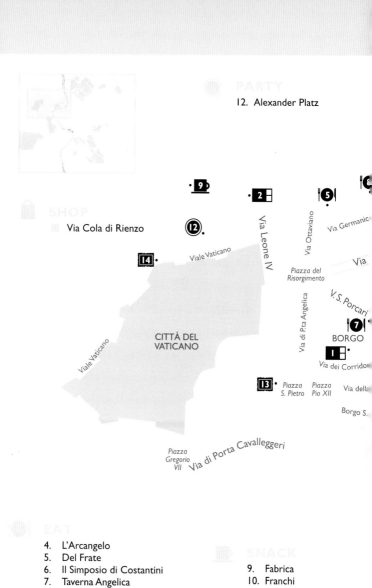

PARTY

12. Alexander Platz

SHOP

Via Cola di Rienzo

Via Germanic

Via Leone IV

Via Ottaviano

Viale Vaticano

Via

Piazza del
Risorgimento

V.S. Porcari

Via di Pta Angelica

CITTÀ DEL
VATICANO

BORGO

Viale Vaticano

Via dei Corrido

Piazza
S. Pietro

Piazza
Pio XII

Via della

Borgo S.

Piazza
Gregorio
VII

Via di Porta Cavalleggeri

Testaccio and Trastevere

South of the river and away from the baroque razzmatazz are Rome's most authentic neighbourhoods.

Postcard-pretty cobbled Trastevere has suffered somewhat from the influx of mass tourism, but it still has unadulterated pockets, especially on the quieter, less inhabited side by Piazza Santa Cecilia where book-shops double up as brunch stops and the air is thick with the mouth-watering scent of mamma's *ragu*. The Trasteverini claim to be the real Romans, descended from 1st-century AD sailors, and you can witness this weather-worn tribe daily in full effect at the rambunctious Bar San Calisto.

In the days of Imperial Rome this area was mostly agricultural, with vil-las, gardens and vineyards for the delectation of the caesars. The majestic leftovers remain in the verdant pastures of the Villa Pamphili park, high up beyond the Janiculum hill, and the Orto Botanico by the river bank.

The main point of entry to Trastevere is via the Ponte Sisto footbridge, built for Pope Sixtus IV but now occupied by a 'no-global' gang of harmless, cider-quaffing hippies complete with dogs on strings and other beg-ging accessories. If you prefer a more mechanical form of trans-port then you'll need to cross the Ponte Garibaldi instead.

ROMA CLUB

Along from Trastevere and under the Aventine hill is the salt-of-the-earth working-class neighbourhood of Testaccio. Once home to a huge slaughterhouse and its workers, this neighbourhood has become a nocturnal hub of clubs and bars. The daily market offers a rare glimpse into authentic everyday Roman life, complete with riotous colours and even more riotously colourful characters.

Opposite the old slaughterhouse, which is now given over to raves, art exhibitions and social activism, is the Monte di Testaccio, a 35m-high hill made from the shards of clay pots, which once upon a time carried provisions into Ancient Rome. Oil and wine were decanted here, and then  the *amphorae* were crushed and slung on the pile, building a hill over time. By the 17th century, wine cellars and *osterie* were burrowing their way into the cool, clay hill and since then have been transformed into bars and nightclubs along Rome's buzziest strip.

Just behind the vast and rather incongruous pyramid of Caio Cestio is the up-and-coming neighbourhood of Ostiense, earmarked for intense renovation. Rem Koolhaus and his architecture clan will be sprucing up the old Mercati Generali to create a retail, culture and leisure development to resemble something like London's Covent Garden. It's now home to the wonderfully forward-thinking Centrale Montemartini, a collection of classical sculpture displayed on and around an old electricity plant. Property prices are now doubling, so enjoy the urban bohemian edge while you still can, and check out the cool clubs around Via Libetta.

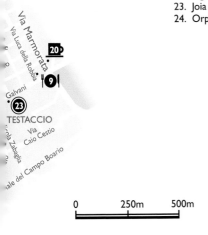

CULTURE
25. Santa Maria
26. Villa Farnesina

PARTY
21. Akab
22. Big Mama's Jazz Club
23. Joia
24. Orpheus

0   250m   500m

Monti, Esquiline & San Lorenzo

Stepping back from the Centro Storico are the layers of Rome that most visitors rarely experience. The Esquiline hill rises from beside the remains of the Roman Forum up to Termini station with Monti on one side and the sleazy chic of San Lorenzo towards the north-east.

Behind Trajanís Market is the delightful neighbourhood of Monti, fast becoming one of the hottest addresses in Rome. So-called because of its undulating landscape of steep cobbled hills, it was once the ëSuburraí in ancient times, a seething, sweaty, noisy pit, home to the urban poor. Now it's an affluent residential neighbourhood; while the Via dei Serpenti and Via del Boschetto quietly pulsate with trendy cafés, bars and boutiques, Monti still retains a calm and distinctively local flavour.

The Colosseum can just be glimpsed at the end of Via dei Serpenti, especially dramatic when illuminated at night. This is a quiet area and home to one of Rome's best new boutique hotels, the Hotel Capo d'Africa.

Up the Esquiline hill and along the flank of Termini station was once filled with ancient ruins and palatial Renaissance villas, but the reunification of Italy in 1870 brought urban planners from Piedmont who swept away the carpet of historical grandeur to make way for a grid like city plan resembling Turin.

Despite various cultural initiatives insisting that the area is undergoing something of a regeneration, it still feels rather slummy, and has something of the immigrant ghetto about it, with wholesale Chinese shops and budget one-star accommodation. The arrival of the monolithic ES hotel (now the Radisson SAS) with its glamorous rooftop pool has kick started these pretensions of rehab, but the immediate locality is less than picturesque and frequented by questionable nocturnal characters. South of the station is distinctively more salubrious, with the ultra luxuriant Hotel Exedra in Piazza della Repubblica.

Just beyond the shabby patch of land north of the station to the east of the city is lively, artsy San Lorenzo. Until recently a no-go area of shady low-life and drug dealers and still badly scarred from consistent bombings in World War II, San Lorenzo is one of the  most interesting neighbourhoods in Rome. Ferociously proletariat and left wing in the '50s and '60s, the area has always been home to artists and socialist intelligentsia, most famously cinematographer and writer Pier Paolo Pasolini.

Little has changed today, and a bohemian brigade of graphic designers, artists and writers have occupied the area's desirable loft accommodation and frequent the neighbourhood's clutch of superb restaurants. Eateries Uno e Bino, Vinarium and Arancia Blu are highly recommended as is the more rustic working-class fodder at Pommidoro and perennial favourite Tram Tram along the tram tracks. Most places are open well into the night, accommodating the bohemian night owls with their irregular timetables.

San Lorenzo is certainly worth a visit for dinner, but don't be appalled by its down-at-heel appearance. It's an area that oscillates violently between grungy on one corner and sophisticated and refined on the next. This is what gives it a cultural edge and makes for a refreshing antidote to the chequered table cloths and cloying tourism in the Centro Storico.

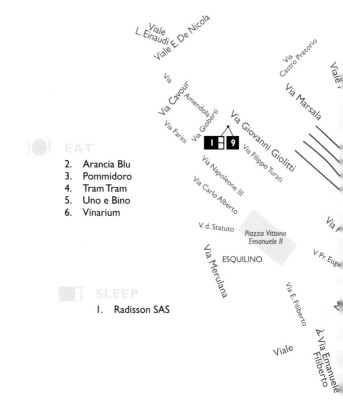

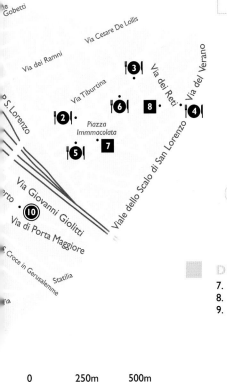

Via Gobetti

Via Cesare De Lollis

Via dei Ramni

Via Tiburtina

Via dei Reti

Via del Verano

③

②

⑥

8

④

Piazza
Immmacolata

7

⑤

P S. Lorenzo

Viale dello Scalo di San Lorenzo

Via Giovanni Giolitti

erto

⑩

Via di Porta Maggiore

S Croce in Gerusalemme

Statilia

ia

PARTY

10. Micca Club

DRINK

7. Arco degli Aurunci
8. Bar a Book
9. Zest

0   250m   500m

sleep...

Hitherto dominated by stuffy baroque palaces, heavy with gilt, brocade and chandeliers, accommodation in Rome has improved dramatically of late, in both range and quality. A new breed of hotels is emerging, run by younger, well-travelled hoteliers and catering to a fashionable clientele rather than the Grand Tour stalwarts lost in some 19th-century fantasy of chintz and high tea.

High-octane luxury is back in a big way, partly thanks to the Boscolo hotel empire's recent additions: the Exedra, and the design-conscious Aleph, both near the Via Veneto. These two are sybaritic temples with heavenly spas.

However, traditional taste needn't mean pompous and staid. The Hotel Eden reeks of sophistication and traditional glamour, and the filmstar magnet Hotel de Russie offers impeccable service while remaining terminally chic.

At the other extreme, minimalist hotel styling – Ripa (below), Radisson SAS – has worked to varying degrees of success in Rome (perhaps because it jars so violently with fantasies of the romantic Eternal City), and the stripped-down Schrager aesthetic feels more than a little fatigued these days.

Enter the more personal and lusciously decorated boutique hotels, which provide an antidote to the big chain monoliths, and the spread of chic and unpretentious B&B guesthouses. Daphne Inn and Le Clarisse offer a warm, personal and affordable service without comprising on style.

If you do want the full experience, however (complete with the reassuringly mammoth price tag), it's best to check into somewhere like the Hassler (below), where every caprice will be catered for around the clock.

Take note that there are two particularly fabulous three-star hotels in this collection, which we think deserve a special mention for their services to style – the Locarno and Hotel Adriano.

Hotel rooftop bars are also some of the most chic places in the city to get a drink (try Zest bar at the Radisson SAS, 7th Heaven at the Aleph), with a burgeoning cocktail scene invigorating the fashion set. There is nothing lovelier than gazing out onto Rome's skyline during that gorgeous, golden hour at sundown.

There are still some wonderful secrets, too. On a hot day, drift up to the top of the Radisson SAS, pull up a sunbed by the glittering pool and get stuck into some cocktails. Not many people know it's open to non-residents.

Prices given are the rack rates for a double room in low season to a suite in high season; for better rates visit www.hg2.com.

Our top ten places to stay in Rome are:
1. Hotel de Russie
2. Hotel Eden
3. Hassler
4. Aleph
5. Casa Howard
6. Locarno
7. Radisson SAS
8. Inn at the Forum
9. Hotel Adriano
10. Hotel Capo d'Africa

Our top 5 for style are:
1. Hotel de Russie
2. Aleph
3. Il Palazzatto
4. Portrait Suites
5. Casa Howard

Our top 5 for atmosphere are:
1. Locarno
2. Hotel de Russie
3. Hotel Adriano
4. Il Palazzatto
5. Inn at the Forum

Our top 5 for location are:
1. Raphael
2. Hotel Art
3. Inn at Spanish Steps
4. Hotel de Russie
5. Hotel Ponte Sisto

Abitart, Via P. Matteucci 10, Ostiense

Tel: 06 454 3191   www.abitarthotel.com

Rates: €100–350

Abitart is a little removed from the centre of town (behind the Pyramid on the Via Ostiense), but for those who have already seen the sights and want to explore a cool, up-and-coming part of town, it might be an interesting

choice. The theme here, unsurprisingly, is art. Designed for the *cognoscenti*, rooms are inspired by different artists and movements, including Picasso, Keith Haring and intellectual Russian Deconstructivism. The adjoining restaurant, Estrobar, is a trendy cocktail hotspot. Exuberantly decorated with contemporary paintings, it's populated by a mostly Roman clientele, chowing down on the elusive (in Rome) *pizza napoletana*.

Style 8, Atmosphere 7, Location 6

Aleph, Via di San Basilio 15, Centro Storico

Tel: 06 422 901   www.boscolohotels.com

Rates: €200–2,000

A temple to city-slick, decadent design, architect Adam Tihany's creation for the Boscolo chain won the prize for Best Hotel Interior Design in Europe in 2004. Love it or hate it, the hotel is built around the theme of saints and sinners, and heaven and hell (we all know which is more fun). Two samurai warriors stand sentinel at the red crystal entrance lobby representing the relative powers of good and evil, but those who choose the heavenly spa will find it in the basement rather than aloft in paradise. Duly cleansed and purified, you will then discover that all manner of naughtiness is invited in the lift as you soar up to the upper levels. Some may complain that the design slips into self-consciousness and that Aleph is too saturated with

detail, so if you like your interiors discreet it may not be the place for you. Intense and brooding red and black dominate the communal spaces, but the rooms are less aggressive and have a more soothing, neutral palette with 1930s- and '40s-inspired Italian design furnishings. Even if you're not staying in the hotel, a cocktail at the 7th Heaven rooftop bar is a sexy date, and the day spa is open to non-residents.

Style 9, Atmosphere 8, Location 8

Bramante, Vicolo delle Palline 24, Prati
Tel: 06 6880 6426   www.hotelbramante.com
Rates: €110–245

For dedicated hedonists who want to stay near the Vatican, the choices are unfortunately fairly limited, with a measly offering of hotels and quality restaurants. The Bramante stands out in this otherwise barren area for its simple but comfortable rooms and location a mere 100m from St Peter's – it has been offering hospitality to pilgrims since 1873. It may only be a humble three stars but the restored rooms are indisputably elegant with high-beamed wooden ceilings, wrought-iron beds and some fairly charming views over the internal courtyard. Triple and quadruple rooms are also available,

and service is cordial and consummate.

Style 7, Atmosphere 7, Location 8

Casa Howard, Via Sistina 149, Centro Storico
Tel: 06 6992 4555
Rates: €150–230

Another chic-boutique B&B, Casa Howard occupies two locations, both in historical *palazzi* near the Spanish Steps. At Via Capo le Case furnishings and décor seek to recreate all the comfort of staying in a contemporary English country house, with parquet floors, oil paintings and antiques. At Via Sistina

the styling is more eclectic, with exotic themes: there's the Zebra room, for instance, with its retina-bending black-and-white stripes, or the Chinese room draped in Shanghai silks. The nature of the old buildings means that quarters can be a little cramped and not all rooms have their own bathroom. However, this shouldn't put you off: kimonos and slippers are provided for those who have to creep down the corridor. A Turkish *hammam* steam bath is available in each location (for an extra charge). Fresh flowers from Frascati and soaps from the Renaissance apothecary Officina Profumo di Santa Maria Novella, as well as fresh croissants and Tuscan jam, are blissful personal touches. Additional services from hairdressing to a massage can be arranged on request.

Style 8, Atmosphere 8, Location 8

Capo d'Africa, Via Capo d'Africa 54, Via Veneto
Tel: 06 772 801/06 594 848 www.hotelcapodafrica.com
Rates: €300–500

Tucked behind the Colosseum on a quiet, mellow street, the Capo d'Africa has all the makings of a modern design classic, but lacks the intimidating high style of some other fashionable hotels. Behind the elegant façade flanked with palm trees, the 64 rooms and communal spaces are decorated

with soft honey wood furnishings and a mellow palette of colours, keeping things crisp yet cosy. Nods to contemporary art – such as the wall of black rubber rose buds – are creative without being overpowering. Some may complain that the hotel is a little far from the centre of town, but it depends on where you want to be and how frenetic you feel. Notably it's just around the corner from one of Rome's under-visited archaeological attractions, the Basilica di San Clemente. Highlights include the romantic roof terrace, dripping with jasmine and honeysuckle, with atmospheric views of the Colosseum and the medieval church Santi Quattro Coronati at night.

Style 8, Atmosphere 8, Location 8

Cavalieri Hilton, Via Alberto Cadlolo 101, Prati

Tel: 06 35 091 www.cavalieri-hilton.it

Rates: €675–1,085

Redolent of Las Vegas kitsch, the Cavalieri Hilton is possibly the most spectacularly vulgar hotel in all of Rome. Set in 15 acres of land on the unofficial eighth hill of Rome, it is rather removed from the centre (you'll require a shuttle bus service to reach anything vaguely interesting), but it does have

panoramic views over the whole city. Lacking in contemporary sophistication, this hotel feels like a cruise liner bound for the island of crass. If you like glitzy Euro-trash and want to flash your money in *nouveau-riche* heaven then you'll absolutely love it. Huge plasma screens clash with the gaudy baroque furnishings in the bedrooms while the pool attracts a pantheon of international plutocrats swimming in their own misguided taste. It's not without its redeeming features, however, including super-chef Heinz Beck's Michelin-starred rooftop restaurant La Pergola, and its unparalleled facilities: a top-notch spa with La Prairie products, an excellent gym, two tennis courts and the Olympic-sized pool – the perfect backdrop for quaffing *pina-coladas*. Just *perfetto* for a clientele that is executive, opulent and diplomatic. If you want to relive the last, excessive days of the Roman Empire à la Nero, then this is the place to do it.

Style 6, Atmosphere 7, Location 6

Daphne Inn, Daphne Veneto, 55 Via di San Basilico, Via Veneto Tel: 06 4782 3529
Daphne Trevi, 20 Via degli Avignonesi, Via Veneto
Tel: 06 4544 9177 www.daphne-rome.com
Rates: €80–520

At the vanguard of the new breed of unpretentious boutique B&Bs, Daphne Inn has two very central locations – you can get from one to the other in the time it takes to eat a *gelato* around Piazza Barberini. Guests can come and go as they please, which makes this ideal for those who want a more discreet, understated experience with none of the gilt and pomp of some of

Rome's five-star hotels. Crisp linens and Simmons mattresses are complemented by cream and earthy tones in the bedrooms, and an abundant breakfast buffet is served in the cosy breakfast lounge. Young couple Elyssa and Alesandro pride themselves on a personalized service and provide mobile phones for guests to contact them for round-the-clock assistance. All rooms at Daphne Veneto have en-suite bathrooms, while at Daphne Trevi some are shared.

Style 7, Atmosphere 8, Location 8

Eden, Via Ludovisi 49, Via Veneto
Tel: 06 478121 www.hotel-eden.it
Rates: €460–3,500

A palpable sense of tradition and glamour embraces you as soon as you step through the door of the lovely Hotel Eden. Since 1889 a string of illustrious guests, including actors, politicians and royalty 'wintering in Rome', have been spoiled with the same attention to detail and timeless luxury. The cream, navy and wicker furnishings and décor cater to a decidedly Anglophile taste, and the overall atmosphere is that of an English country home, with carefully placed oil paintings and repro furniture. Rooms them-

selves are a relaxing combination of creams and quality fabrics in refined colours. Book a room on the fifth floor for a private balcony overlooking the trees of nearby Villa Borghese. The top-floor, Michelin-starred restaurant is a luxuriant and unforgettable treat. Be warned: if romance is on the cards then a *prosecco* on the gorgeous terrace, which boasts one of the most spectacular panoramic views of the whole of Rome, could get you making all sorts of promises.

Style 9, Atmosphere 9, Location 9

Exedra, Piazza della Repubblica 47, Monti
Tel: 06 489 381 www.boscolohotels.com
Rates: €450–3,500

Probably Rome's best example of glam-slam luxury, the Exedra sweeps unapologetically across the entire corner of the Piazza della Repubblica, facing the baths of Diocletian. The 240 rooms range from (extremely high) standard classic to outrageously glamorous executive suites resembling the type of phenomenal Manhattan apartments you only see on *Sex in the City*. The Exedra outshone the rest of the cast in its recent celluloid appearance in the film *Ocean's Twelve*, but the cinematic references don't stop there – the ground-floor Tazio champagne bar is named after and inspired by the paparazzo photographer of the same name in *La Dolce Vita*, while the first

floor houses La Frustra restaurant in homage to Fellini's 1963 film *8/2*. Looking out over the Eternal City is the jaw-droppingly sexy rooftop pool, which hangs over the edge of Piazza della Repubblica and the Fountain of the Naidi. When the sun doesn't shine the prestigious indoor spa provides plenty of pampering. The hotel is very close to Termini station and excellently located for the gorgeous Monti district, but getting into town requires a bus or walk down the Via Nazionale traffic promenade.

Style 8, Atmosphere 8, Location 7

Forty Seven, Via Luigi Petroselli 47, Ripa
Tel: www.fortysevenhotel.com
Rates: €290–550

Located just along from the Bocca della Verita (the famous 'Mouth of Truth'),

tucked behind the Campidoglio, Forty Seven's position on a busy traffic artery may seem a little uncomfortable. But with easy access to Trastevere and Testaccio and the Centro just a 10-minute walk, this hotel – housed in a former Fascist building – is well worth considering. Chic yet unassuming, it has a freshness that some of the city's design-conscious establishments lack. The décor, wood and marble, with fairly masculine styling softened by injections of colourful flowers, make a clean break from the chintz without going too far in the minimalist direction. Each of the five floors pays tribute to a different 20th-century Italian artist, from Modigliani to Umberto Mastroianni and Piero Guccione. Take in the gorgeous sunsets over a cocktail and dinner at the restaurant Circus in the roof garden.

Style 8, Location 7, Atmosphere 8

Grand Hotel de la Minerve, Piazza della Minerva 69, Centro Storico

Tel: 06 695 201 www.grandhoteldelaminerve.it
Rates: €375–1,700

Once an ecclesiastical 17th-century *palazzo*, then a Grand Tour hotel stalwart, the Grand Hotel de la Minerve is more than a little dated these days. However, its central location by the Pantheon and the magnificent roof

terrace make the cringingly 1970s upholstery in the atrium a little more palatable. Don't be put off by the entrance hall, presided over by a marble statue of the Roman goddess Minerva – despite the gaudy chandeliers and staid furnishings the actual rooms are a little more up to date, with pinches of contemporary art and more modish lighting. The presidential suites really hit the mark, with revamped luxury styling and detail. If you avoid the tacky dining rooms and restaurant (with some of the best eateries on your doorstep, it's no sacrifice), this hotel makes a practical and pleasing choice. Play 'spot the church domes' from the flower-festooned roof terrace over a €15 Americano cocktail, if that's your bag, or while away the balmy evening drifting off to some piano music. It's the stuff that cheesy holiday dreams are made of. You won't find the bright young things of Rome here, but it has its own naïve sort of charm.

Style 7, Location 9, Atmosphere 7

Hassler Roma, Piazza Trinita dei Monti 6, Via Veneto

Tel: 06 699 340 www.hotelhassler.com
Rates: €410–3,200

This fifth-generation Swiss hotel, which was requisitioned by the US air force to serve as their HQ during World War II, crowns the top of the Spanish Steps. The style is bombastically luxuriant, with plush carpets, sweeping staircases and chandeliers, but it resists descending into über-baroque.

The rooms are all unique (with their individual touches coming courtesy of owner Robert Wirth's wife), but nevertheless remain in keeping with the same sumptuous European elegance that is evident throughout. They are a bit chintzy and gilded, but think parquet as opposed to fusty carpet, and marble bathrooms are standard. The Palm Court Garden is a civilized take on the English country garden, while a few *beau-monde* characters inhabit the Salone Eva, puffing on cigars or necking a few post-theatre sherries. The emphasis here is on service, and the Hassler makes grand claims that it tries to satisfy every capricious whim of its guests – so if you want cherry cola at 4am, you may just be in luck. The hotel also offers a Dan Brown-inspired Angels and Demons luxury package. As Miss Jean Brody would say, 'for those who like that sort of thing, that is the sort of thing they like'.

Style 9, Atmosphere 8, Location 9

Hotel Adriano, Via di Pallacorda 2, Centro Storico
Tel: 06 6880 2451 www.hoteladriano.com
Rates: €110–300

A recent revamp from arbiter of style Barbara Ricci has left this gem of a hotel one of the hottest new addresses in Rome. A family business for over 40 years, the Hotel Adriano is certainly worthy of more stellar accolades than it has received. The 80 rooms are comfortably stylish with eclectic,

decorative touches – Barbara's travels throughout various subcontinents give the rooms and lobby an idiosyncratic and original touch. Pretty botanical drawings and interesting details adorn the bathrooms, and the bar in the lobby resembles a funky souk. The hotel occupies part of a 16th-century *palazzo*, nestling in an atmospheric labyrinth of cobbled streets behind the Pantheon and Piazza Navona. An opening party attended by Rome's glitterati in spring 2006 has cemented its status as one of the sexy new kids on the block. Really, really cool.

Style 9, Atmosphere 9, Location 9

Hotel Art, Via Margutta 56, Centro Storico
Tel: 06 328 711 www.hotelart.it
Rates: €284–950

This appropriately named hotel lurks on the lovely Via Margutta, a street that was stuffed to the gills with artists' studios back in the 1600s. Take one look at the lobby and you'll notice that here Rome's artistic heritage has decidedly fast-forwarded to the contemporary. In fact you might even say

audaciously so when you first see white space pods like giant snowballs housing the reception desk, and eye-watering splashes of orange, yellow, green and blue along the corridors. Rooms are decorated in a softer, neutral palette with dark wood, but can be a little cramped, and the novelty factor of being on a pseudo-spaceship may pall after a while. The enduring attraction of this hotel however, is its location, smack bang in the centre of town yet a real sanctuary from the crowds around the nearby Spanish Steps and Via del Corso.

Style 8, Atmosphere 8, Location 9

Hotel Ponte Sisto, Via dei Pettinari 64, Centro Storico
Tel: 06 686 310 www.hotelpontesisto.it
Rates: €180–420

Hotel Ponte Sisto sits neatly on the edge of the river, just by the eponymous bridge, in a delectable restored Renaissance *palazzo*. Rooms are simply fitted and a little anaemic-looking, but all are kitted out with sumptuous marble bathrooms for that hint of Roman opulence. The palm-lined internal courtyard is the real treat here, and makes a gorgeous backdrop for break-

fast or an *aperitivo*. It may feel a little anonymous and business-like in some respects, but its proximity to all the best evening distractions is a real boon. The Vatican and St Peter's are also a picturesque walk away along the ivy-curtained Via Giulia.

Style 7, Atmosphere 8, Location 9

Hotel de Russie, Via del Babuino 9, Centro Storico
Tel: 06 328 881   www.hotelderussie.it
Rates: €420–2,700

When filmstars are in town they make a beeline for the Hotel de Russie, so expect a constant herd of paparazzi waiting to pounce as the limousines roll

by. Part of the Rocco Forte hotel group, it's a far cry from the cloying chintz and gilt of other luxury hotels and its dramatic location on the corner of Piazza del Popolo has cemented its status as one of Rome's most popular hotels. Rooms are a polished affair with 1930s-style décor, luxurious linens and pretty mosaic-tiled bathrooms. The courtyard overlooking sweeping terraces and verdant gardens is a cool haven at anytime of day, and a precious spot for an upper-crust cocktail (see Drink).

Style 9, Location 9, Atmosphere 8

Hotel Sant'Anselmo, Piazza di Sant'Anselmo 2, Trastevere
Tel: 06 570 057 www.aventinohotels.com
Rates: €180–240

Its tranquil and romantic position on the leafy Aventine hill makes the Hotel Sant'Anselmo a mellow refuge rather than a place for a high-octane party weekend. Rooms are ostentatiously styled with dramatic four-poster beds and decadent touches such as free-standing baths in some, although at times the décor feels a little naïve. A recent refurbishment has seen the addition of a huge column of Swarovski crys-tals in the stairwell, casting fragments of rainbows onto the chintzy sofas. In summer the relaxing terrace, with its idyllic views of the 5th-century churches Sant'Anselmo and Santa Sabina next door, is a pleasant spot.

Style 7, Atmosphere 7, Location 7

Inn at the Forum, Via degli Ibernesi 30, Monti
Tel: 06 6919 0970   www.theinnattheromanforum.com
Rates: €210–1,400

The paint is still drying at this newly opened hotel in a quiet backstreet of
Monti, but whoever judges these things was sufficiently impressed to bestow
a small luxury hotel award on the Di Renzo brothers in 2006. An unassuming front door leads off the residential street into this quietly fabulous

establishment, with 12 rooms touched by the magic of the Hotel de Russie's
designer. Contemporary opulence dominates the décor, with crystal chandeliers and lavish fabrics. Particular details – for example, iPod speakers in all
the rooms – help to make this boutique hotel stand out, but the real jewel
in its crown is the internal walled garden on the top floor, with fig, olive and
lemon trees backing onto two resplendent 'executive suites'. Uniquely, an
original Roman subterranean crypt from the remains of Trajan's marketplace
has been excavated on the ground floor, making a cool refuge when the
temperature soars. Breakfast is served in a lounge area or on the intimate
panoramic terrace overlooking the atmospheric ruins of the Roman Forum.
To cap it all, it is perfectly situated for enjoying the hip Monti neighbourhood.

Style 9, Location 9, Atmosphere 8

Inn at Spanish Steps, Via dei Condotti 85, Centro Storico
Tel: 06 699 25657   www.atspanishsteps.com
Rates: €240–750

A pleasant alternative to the stuffy hotel palaces that line the Via Condotti and the Spanish Steps, the 'Inn' has a luxury boutique feel while still managing to retain that comforting patina of old-world charm. And since it's right in the throbbing heart of the city's designer shopping promenade, it's ideal for those on a retail binge. The 22 rooms are plushly decorated with elaborate damask and animal-hide furnishings, and some have original fireplaces and ornately frescoed ceilings. Staff are helpful and there's a civilized lounge and terrace where you can take tea and wallow in the newspapers (and credit card receipts).

Style 8, Atmosphere 8, Location 9

In Town, Via Bocca di Leone 7, Centro Storico

Tel: 06 6938 0200   www.intownroma.it
Rates: €300–800

A brand new luxury townhouse hotel right in the shopping triangle – perfect for those who want to be next door to Marni and a stone's-throw from the legendary Roman nightclub Gilda. The townhouse comprises six

minimalist suites in a Japanese-inspired décor of pebbles, cactus plants and a muted palette of cream, greys and browns, all equipped with the ubiquitous plasma screens. Its size gives this boutique guesthouse discreet, private and decidedly grown-up feel, but it could seem a little cold for some tastes – think 1980s bachelor pad – clean and crisp rather than romantic and whimsical. Don't attempt the lift unless you live on a diet of sushi, it's slimmer than the latest in mobile phone technology.

Style 8, Atmosphere 7, Location 9

Locarno, Via delle Penna 22, Centro Storico
Tel: 06 361 0841 www.locarno.com
Rates: €150–650

Consistently popular and desperately romantic despite its surprising three-star status, the Locarno delivers well to all budgets. There's a distinct feeling of clandestine capers going on behind the wooden doors and illicit kisses in the perilous birdcage lift, a leftover from the building's first incarnation as a

five-star hotel in 1925. Run with an iron rod by the matriarch Caterina Valente, the Locarno has 48 rooms in the older building, but for unrivalled, sumptuous romance get a suite next door, in the restructured Venetian patrician *palazzo*, which is more private and perfect for an amorous weekend. There's also a lovely sun-bleached roof terrace for tea, a chat or a sunbathe. Having accommodated everyone from impoverished artists (such as Michelangelo Pistoletto) to rich lovers, it's no wonder this hotel gives the impression that it is harbouring a few secrets behind its Art Deco walls.

Free bicycles are on offer for the brave.

Style 9, Atmosphere 8, Location 9

Il Palazzetto International Wine Academy, Vicolo del Bottino 8, Via Veneto

Tel: 06 699 0878 www.wineacademyroma.com
Rates: €215–345

This 16th-century *palazzo*, nestling under the wing of the Spanish Steps, belongs to the Hotel Hassler. It also doubles up as the headquarters for the International Wine Academy, presided over by the same prolific Mr Wirth. The concept is legendary, combining the comfort of four delicious boutique hotel rooms with the fine art of wine. The rooms are elegantly decorated in beige and black, and guests can enjoy all the facilities on offer at the adjoining Hotel Hassler. Il Palazzetto feels like a sojourn in a private house rather than in a grand hotel, and its setting is certainly unique. If that wasn't enough the Aroma restaurant and wine bar (see Snack) is a wonderfully

intimate hideaway from the tourist rabble. Chess fans get ready: there's an antique chessboard in the cosy library bar which begs some sexy *tête-à-têtes*. Wine tasting and gastronomy courses are on offer in English, Italian and French, and the Palazzetto also organizes short trips to wine regions for small groups. Could you ask for more?

Style 9, Atmosphere 8, Location 9

Portrait Suites, Via Bocca di Leone 23, Centro Storico
Tel: 06 6938 0742 www.lungarnohotels.com
Rates: €290–720

The latest offering from the luxury Florentine Lungarno hotel group,
Portrait Suites opened above the Ferragamo men's shop on the corner of
Via Condotti in July 2006. The hotelier's first foray out of Florence and into
Rome is a glamorous townhouse comprising 14 rooms, 8 studios, 5 suites
and a penthouse. Idiosyncratic touches include an open fire on the terrace

and an honesty bar. Luxury fabrics such as boar skin cover the tables and
lifts and reflect the sybaritic Ferragamo brand, while marble floors and
black-and-white photos of iconic fashion moments keep the atmosphere
youthful.

Style 9, Atmosphere 8, Location 9

Radisson SAS, Via F Turati, 171, Monti
Tel: 06 444 841 www.rome.radissonsas.com
Rates: €185–1,800

When it first opened in 2002, this huge Schrager-esque monolith behind
Termini station caused ripples through Rome's fashion set. After falling into
the hands of the Radisson group, there is a slightly more corporate feel, but
unusually it hasn't suffered too much under the clutches of a franchise. The
concept is industrial chic, which goes rather well with the down-at-heel
location, overlooking the train tracks. Rooms are pared down, with a

slate-grey palette and techno features such as DVD players and plasma screens and a multifunctional control for curtains, lighting and appliances. A glass screen separates the low platform beds from the bathroom. With all that monotone the multicoloured neon lighting under the windows at night is a welcome respite. The hotel comes into its own come summer when the Miami-style rooftop pool opens, while all year round the top floor bar is a lively affair with a mean line in punchy cocktails.

Style 8, Atmosphere 8, Location 8

Raphael, Largo Febo 2, Centro Storico
Tel: 06 682 831   www.raphaelhotelrome.com
Rates: €260–2,000

The Raphael hotel sits under a romantic curtain of ivy bedecked with fairy lights in a quiet corner just behind Piazza Navona. Despite being a favourite with diplomats and politicians the atmosphere is far from stuffy. The lobby is festooned with eclectic decorations, including original Picasso ceramics and an antique sleigh. Executive rooms on the third floor are

designed by architect-du-jour Richard Meier and resemble classy Nordic houses with warm oak furnishings and bathrooms in Carrara marble. It's also perfectly situated for exploring the golden triangle of backstreets, wine bars and *vicoli* between Piazza Navona and the river, home to many of the city's best watering-holes (Societe Lutece, Bar della Pace, Bar del Fico; see Drink). The Raphael is also next door to the wonderful Santa Lucia restaurant, although the rooftop restaurant here on the fabulous roof terrace is a delight.

Style 8, Atmosphere 8, Location 10

Relais Le Clarisse, Via Cardinale Merry du Val, Trastevere
Tel: 06 5833 4437 www.leclarisse.com
Rates: €130–280

This unpretentious guesthouse is a welcome addition to Trastevere, where accommodation is scarce. The five simple rooms all face onto a communal internal courtyard, which was once the cloister of the ancient convent of Santa Chiara, bedecked with fresh-smelling herbs and plants. It may feel a lit-

tle Spartan compared with other Roman hotels but its location more than compensates. The rooms are cosy, clean and crisp, and service is warm and helpful. Good for the summer months and for those who want to get on with doing their own thing, even if that just means pootling around Trastevere drinking cappuccinos all day.

Style 7, Location 9, Atmosphere 7

Ripa, Via degli Orti di Trastevere 1, Trastevere
Tel: 06 58 611 www.ripahotel.com
Rates: €155–500

It's Rome's first foray into modern hotel design, and the 1990s minimalism of Ripa Hotel may be too severe for some tastes. Slightly shabby from outside, the inside is friendly and warm and the bold red sofas inject some colour. Rooms are comfortable, if a little too pared down (with monchrome shades and minibars covered in black velvet hanging from the walls). The location, in an unkempt corner of Trastevere, is slightly peripheral, but if you

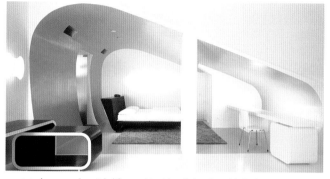

want to be near the nightlife on this side of the river it's fairly convenient. Since the Op Art-styled adjoining nightclub La Suite closed its doors, the hotel's fashion credentials have slipped slightly. However, there's a bit of a scene at the neighbouring Ripartcafé, which hosts regular live music evenings and starts to buzz at lunchtimes and the *aperitivo* hour. A rather hit and miss   experience.

Style 8, Location 7, Atmosphere 7

Rome Palace, Via Veneto 70, Via Veneto
Tel: 06 478 719 www.boscolohotels.com
Rates: €180–2,200

You can feel an air of simple, tranquil luxury as soon as you walk through the door of this four-star hotel on the Via Veneto. Rooms are tastefully decorated in a 1920s ocean-liner style, and the hotel boasts one of the best

spas in Rome, with a glorious Art Deco pool. The hotel has an interesting
history, partly due to its location in front of the American Embassy, which

drew ambassadors into the Art Deco lounge for meetings during World
War II. Prior to that, the hotel was a key landmark in Rome's *dolce vita* days
– the piano bar/salon, decorated with frescoes immortalizing the high
society of the 1930s, was often frequented for a cocktail or two by Fellini
himself.

Style 8, Atmosphere 8, Location 8

St Regis Grand, Vittorio Emanuele Orlando 3, Via Veneto
Tel: 06 47091 www.stregis.com/grandrome
Rates: €300–1,250

Unapologetically pompous and kitsch, the St Regis hotel queens it up to
lavish effect. Nautically dressed genteel ladies populate the lobby with their
monogrammed luggage, and slightly sneering concierges add to the fun. This
hotel is from a bygone age and perhaps takes first place in the baroque
brigade of Rome's hotels. It takes itself a little too seriously – but then again
has won a place on Condé Nast Traveller's Gold List. Tea is meticulously
served in the sparkling, chandeliered salon and consists of scones, slightly
stale sandwiches and delicious biscuits and petits fours. The St Regis should
be approached with a sense of humour by the modern visitor, but you know
your grandmother would love it. Amenities include a 24-hour concierge
service, business centre, well-equipped gym and full-scale butler service in
all of the 23 suites.

Style 7/8, Atmosphere 7, Location 7

View at Spanish Steps, Via dei Condotti 91, Centro Storico
Tel: 06 6992 5657   www.theviewatthespanishsteps.com
Rates: €480–3,500

A more luxuriant sister to the Inn at the Spanish Steps, whose four rooms occupy the penthouse of the same *palazzo* and offer a more exclusive serv-

ice. Plasma screens, jacuzzis and marble bathrooms come as standard, with a 24-hour butler on demand and a personal chef on request. Guests can enjoy the intimacy of being in their own private apartment right in the heat of the action but still enjoy the luxury service of a five-star-plus hotel. If there's a group seeking a sybaritic play palace for a few nights, why not book the penthouse? There's a heavenly terrace made for quaffing *prosecco* overlooking the Spanish Steps.

Visconti Palace, Via Federico Cesi 37, Prati

Tel: 06 3684 www.viscontipalace.com

Rates: €116–266

From the outside the Visconti Palace looks a bit like a 1970s conference centre – all brutalist architecture and heavy concrete – but a recent renovation has made the lobby really rather glamorous, with exotic flowers, brightly coloured furniture and contemporary design lighting. Its location in the well-heeled residential area of Prati is quiet and restful, and yet the hotel is

just a short skip from Piazza del Popolo in the centre of town and the Vatican. Bedrooms still retain a slightly corporate feel, but they're slowly doing them up and have joined the nascent trend in arty Roman hotels, displaying their own (fairly mediocre) collection of 20th-century Italian art.

Style 7, Atmosphere 7, Location 8

eat...

The gastronomic delights of Rome are an absolute odyssey, and nigh on impossible to sample comprehensively in one visit. Rome has mostly resisted the influx of high-fashion restaurants that you might find in Milan. The pleasure of food is largely unadulterated, and gourmet experiences are focused on food rather than kowtowing to a fashionable clientele – some of the trendiest places are often the most ostensibly down-at-heel.

They say that you are what you eat, and the indigenous cuisine certainly defines the Roman character – strong, pure and full of character. Traditional Roman fare is visceral and earthy, with *abbachio alla romana* (lamb with anchovy, garlic, rosemary), *coda alla vaccinara* (oxtail) and *saltimbocca alla romana* (skewered veal roll stuffed with ham, cheese and sage). Pasta staples include the ubiquitous *bucatini all'amatriciana*, with pork cheek, tomato and pecorino, or the simple but delicious *cacio e pepe*, with lashings of black pepper and grated pecorino cheese. Offal and all the leftover bits of the beast are traditional to Roman cuisine and best left to the brave. For the full carnivorous experience you'll have to head over to rustic *trattorie* in Testaccio.

Eateries break down into a rather confusing hierarchy of categories – *osterie* and *trattorie* are historically speaking the most traditional and cheapest establishments, where *cucina tipica* fed a working-class clientele with a rather rough-and-ready service. While there are plenty of examples of these, it's no longer a watertight definition: many *osterie* have become rather glamorous and exclusive (Hosteria del Pesce and Ostaria dell'Orso are a couple of examples with high price tags) but like to think they still true to their roots.

At the top of the chain is the *ristorante*, or restaurant, where you can expect *alta cucina* gourmet dining with a full-on service (but with the mercurial Romans this is not always necessarily a guarantee). *Enoteche*, *cantine* and *vinerie* are technically speaking wine bars – temples to wine that serve accompanying snacks of ham and cheese – but a popular trend has seen the addition of accomplished, innovative cuisine (see Enoteca Ferrara, Vinarium, Uno e Bino), making them the city's most fashionable hotspots.

Creative fusion cooking is slowly on the rise (again fairly provincial tastes have an inhibitive effect) to a varied, but mostly enthusiastic reception. Of particular note is Glass Hostaria in Trastevere. Don't neglect the pull of an atmospheric

pizzeria. When done well, and washed down with a beer or some honest wine, it's one of the most exquisite meals you can have. Da Baffetto and Montecarlo are both well worth considering.

Going off piste (i.e. non-Italian) isn't really a good idea in Rome, since culinary xenophobia tends to dominate.

However, sushi has made its mark on the city and of course Italians love it for its low-fat credentials. Zen Sushi is a favourite, both for quality and style.

Restaurants generally start serving at around 8pm (*pizzerie* from 7pm), so suppress your hunger with a cocktail and a buffet of snacks at *aperitivo* hour (6.30pm onwards). The standard course at meal times is *antipasto* (hors d' oeuvre), *primo* (pasta, soup or risotto), *secondo* (meat or fish dish), *contorno* (a side portion of salad or vegetables) and then *dolce* (dessert).

Prices shown are for three courses and a half bottle of wine, but if you manage all of the above regularly you're a braver soul than I am.

Top 10 restaurants in Rome:
1. Il Pagliaccio
2. Trattoria
3. Santa Lucia
4. La Terazza
5. Maccheroni
6. Antico Arco
7. L'Arcangelo
8. La Rosetta
9. Ostaria dell'Orso
10. Hosteria del Pesce

Top 5 restaurants for food:
1. Il Pagliaccio
2. L'Arcangelo
3. Trattoria
4. Da Enzo
5. Antico Arco

Top 5 restaurants for service:
1. La Terazza
2. Baby
3. Il Pagliaccio
4. Ostaria dell'Orso
5. La Rosetta

Top 5 restaurants for atmosphere:
1. Maccheroni
2. Tutti Frutti
3. Santa Lucia
4. Gusto
5. Il Boom

Al Bric, Via del Pellegrino 51, Centro Storico

Tel: 06 687 9533   www.bric.it

Open: 7.30–11.30pm. Closed Mondays. €40

Italian

This quietly fabulous restaurant and wine bar is tucked away behind the raucous Campo dei Fiori. Inside is a cosy affair with exposed brick and idiosyncratic decorative details, which give you the impression that this is a genuinely secret find. Wine merchant Roberto Marchetti's family has been in

the game for four generations, and the expertise shows with the 1,000 strong selection of wines. The menu is firmly orientated around the combined pleasures of cheese and wine, which slip down wonderfully with the home-made grissini breadsticks. Creative and mouth-watering pasta and risotto feature on the seasonal menu, and certainly do not disappoint. Frequented by a mature Italian cognoscenti crowd who are serious about their *vino*, and other harbingers of culinary taste. Booking is highly recommended, and the dining rooms are deliciously cosy in winter.

Food 8, Service 8, Atmosphere 8

Antico Arco, Piazzale Aurelio 7, Trastevere

Tel: 06 581 5274   www.anticoarco.it

Open: 8pm–midnight. Closed Sundays. €60

Italian

Although a little out of the way, at the top of the Gianicolo (near the Doria

Pamphilj park), Antico Arco is well worth the short taxi ride up to the top of Via Garibaldi. Set in a renovated villa, this warm and modern restaurant creates the feel of dining in a private home, especially in the cosy attic room upstairs. This is added to with the home-made selection of breads and the

excellent house olive oil. Dishes are considered and carefully created to delicious effect while service is competent and convivial without being too overbearing. And a chilled-out, loungey background soundtrack strikes the right note between trendy and classy. Rather than getting a taxi back, amble down the Via Garibaldi on your descent and navigate the couples *in flagrante delictorum* for one of Rome's most romantic panoramas. With the dramatic arch of San Pancrazio behind you (home to regular summer street parties), take the steep stairs on the left (stilettos/ joints permitting) which lead right down into Trastevere's warren of streets for a post-supper *passeggiata* and a spot of bar-hopping. It's popular with staff from the nearby American University and a predominantly Italian crowd, so be sure to book to secure a table.

Food 8, Service 9, Atmosphere 8

Arancia Blu, Via dei Latini 65, San Lorenzo
Tel: 06 445 105
Open: 8pm–midnight daily   €45
Vegetarian

A very friendly establishment with dark wood tables, and an interior embellished with interesting decorative touches. Since it's an *enoteca* the walls are

of course laden with bottles, and the intelligentsia clientele may account for the 'difficult jazz' soundtrack. The menu is creative vegetarian but lacks the pretensions and anxiety often felt in other vegetarian-focused diners, and is surprisingly trendy given that until recently to be vegetarian in Italy marked you out as some sort of culinary leper. Hence the dream of chef and creator Fabio Bassano, who wanted to change the reputation of vegetarian food as a boring and punitive experience. Meat is replaced with lots of pastas, gnocchi and risottos, and the main courses incorporating vegetables in a meat substitute sort of way achieve their aim to varying degrees of success. A spectacular offering of rum and chocolate makes for triumphant desserts. Not a good idea if you are avoiding carbs.

Food 7, Service 7, Atmosphere 8

L'Arcangelo, Via GG belli 59, Prati

Tel: 06 321 0992   www.ristorantidiroma.com/arcangelo
Open: 1–2.30pm, 8–11.30pm. Closed Saturday lunch and Sundays.   €70
Italian – Roman

Sommelier and owner Arcangelo Dandini opened this elegant *trattoria* at the end of 2003 with his wife Stefania, and has since received great acclaim on account of Tuscan chef Fulvio Pierangelini's innovative takes on Roman cuisine. This means a seasonal menu, which leans heavily towards the '*quinto quarto*' dishes – or the leftover butcher's cuts that were given to slaughterhouse workers. So expect intensely flavoured meaty dishes and traditional recipes from the Jewish quarter, such as the famed Roman artichokes and salt cod *baccala*', alongside pasta classics *cacio e pepe* and *amatriciana*. Notably there's a foie gras selection and some unusual discoveries on the wine list to spice things up a bit. Décor has a 1950s feel with wood panelling and classy retro lighting. This place is a temple to gastronomy, with starched linen tablecloths creating a rather rarefied atmosphere, but the

soft jazz soundtrack and convivial air of the regulars softens any stuffiness that may afflict such a place. A mature crowd of gourmands come back over and over again, lauding it with the mantle of best Roman restaurant, so they must be doing something right.

Food 9, Service 8, Atmosphere 8

Baby, Via Ulisse Aldrovandi 15, Rome

Tel: 06 322 3993 www.aldrovandi.com/en/dining.asp
Open: 12.30–2.30pm, 7.30–10.30pm. Closed Mondays.   €80
Italian

If you can't make it to the Amalfi coast, this restaurant, set in the poolside garden of the Aldovrandi Palace hotel, may be the next best thing for some enchanted evening under the stars. Michelin-starred Sorrento chef Alfonso Iaccarino's self-consciously contemporary Baby is visually rather impressive (even if it jars slightly with the 19th-century surroundings of the hotel). Its location makes for as romantic and secluded a dining experience as you can get, with excellent attention to detail and very sprightly and helpful sommeliers. However, while the cuisine is very clearly accomplished, we felt that there are restaurants more worthy of Michelin's stellar accolades. You'll

need a short taxi ride there and back, but enjoy the journey through the Borghese gardens and prepare for a romantic and quietly glamorous evening.

Food 8, Service 9, Atmosphere 8

Il Boom, Via dei Fienaroli 30a, Trastevere

Tel: 06 589 7196 www.ilboom.it

Open: 7.30pm–midnight daily   €40

Southern Italian

Cute, quirky and tucked away from the tourist fodder in the heart of bohemian Trastevere, is Il Boom. Step through the door into a Sixties time warp, but there's not a whiff of Austin Powers pastiche here – the walls are adorned with photos of passionate *dolce vita* actresses and the restaurant's name recalls the excitement of the post-war economic explosion. Inside it

resembles a catalogue of Sixties design, with vintage magazines, books and furniture, while an original 1959 jukebox belts out a 200-record soundtrack from Patti Pravo to Simon and Garfunkel. An über-cool, young and fashionable crowd knock back *passito* (Sicilian dessert wine) after dinner, and rock out to the retro beats with unadulterated brio. Service is warm and friendly while the Southern Italian-inspired food is fresh if a little unexceptional. This doesn't matter – Il Boom is so much fun it's difficult not to love it.

Food 7, Service 7, Atmosphere 8

Da Baffetto, Via del Governo Vecchio 114, Centro Storico
Tel: 06 686 1617
Open: 6–11pm. Closed Mondays.   €18
Italian – Pizza

Forget everything you know, or thought you knew, about pizza. For many this is the original *pizza romana*, served on metal dishes and so thin and tasty it melts in the mouth, without any stodgy aftermath. They don't take bookings, so arrive early (around 7pm) to avoid the hungry scrum that

forms daily without fail. Inside, long tables seat a motley crew of colourful locals, enthusiastic tourists and fashionistas, perhaps making it one of the few true democratic entities in Rome. Service may be slow, but what's the hurry when you can soak up the atmosphere of the cobbled streets on a balmy night, or cosy up inside cheek-to-cheek with the punters on the same, cramped table? Special.

Food 9, Service 6, Atmosphere 9

Da Enzo, Via dei Vascellari 29, Trastevere

Tel: 06 581 8355

Open: 12.30–3.30pm, 7.30–11.30pm. Closed Sundays. €30

Italian – Roman

On the other, less touristy side of Trastevere this unaffected, homely *trattoria* dishes up some of the best and heartiest pasta in Rome. *Crema di peperoni*

(pasta with creamed red pepper sauce) is the exquisite signature dish, alongside traditional Roman classics with simple, predominant flavours (such as *penne all'amatriciana*). Bowls of pasta arrive on the table in never-decreasing mountains,

so don't expect an express meal but instead enjoy watching a cast of fellow diners who wouldn't seem out of place in a Fellini film. Wash it all down with some honest table wine and save room for some of the best *tiramisu* in Rome. Don't be put off by the brusque and surly service – it's all part of the experience; just be surly back and you'll earn their respect. Take a peek into the kitchen to see worryingly large monoliths of meat in preparation, and finally we've a word of warning: do not attempt lunch here if you have a busy afternoon of sightseeing. You won't make it past the Isola Tiberina before needing a rest.

Food 9, Service 6, Atmosphere 9

Dal Bolognese, Piazza del Popolo 1–2, Centro Storico

Tel: 06 361 1426

Open: 1–3pm, 7.30–11.30pm. Closed Mondays. €60

Italian

Traditional high-end Roman eaterie Dal Bolognese poses no surprises or edgy mystique, but sometimes there's more to life than gritty nouveau-chic.

Politicians, diplomats and film stars flock to this Piazza del Popolo restaurant over and over again to sample classic dishes from Emiglia-Romagna, the motherland of Italian cuisine. So expect stuffed pasta, tortellini *in brodo* and

meaty classics, which, although lacking invention, are technically faultless. The ample terrace affords unrivalled people-watching for al fresco diners, but this restaurant and its cuisine come into their own on a damp and chilly night when you're less concerned about your bikini silhouette. Here you'll find a traditional 'Grand Tour'-style service with simpering waiters, classic luxury and a price tag to match. Look for the sports cars parked outside – it might mean Valentino's in town.

Food 9, Service 9, Atmosphere 8

Del Frate, Via degli Scipioni 118, Prati
Tel: 06 323 6437
Open: noon–3pm, 6–11.30pm daily   €50
International

From the outside Del Frate looks like a dusty old *enoteca*, but once you're through the door things are refreshingly modern, clean and fresh. Perfect for a good-value lunch stop (with limited menu) after you have suffered the tourist rabble at the Vatican. The menu expands come evening and offers up a civilized and fulfilling dinner in a romantic setting. For those who like *carpaccio* there's plenty of marinated raw meat and fish to sample, and of course, because it's Prati, evenings see an experimental sushi menu. The *à la carte* is seasonal and traditional (no nasty surprises, yet a few creative

touches), and a whole list dedicated to different chocolate desserts. Eight hundred wines and an enthusiastic selection of whiskies and grappas mean that you could quite possibly catch a creatively inebriated glimpse of St Peter's on your way home.

Food 8, Service 8, Atmosphere 7

Duke's Bar, Viale Parioli 200, Parioli
Tel: 06 8066 2455   www.dukes.it
Open: 8.30pm–midnight. Cocktail bar 7.30pm–2am. Closed Sundays.   €60
International

'Healthy food and caring feelings' is the catchphrase of this stylish restaurant (these mottos never translate well), set in the posh Parioli district of northern Rome. Despite the ostensibly cheesy sentiments, this Californian-

inspired eatery is a handsome alternative to traditional Italian fare and one of the few restaurants with a credible bar scene. (Watch out for the incredibly strong Martinis). It's part of the 'Casual Fine Dining Movement', and chef Massimiliano Iannozzi reworks Californian cuisine. Confused as to what to expect? Fresh, seasonal variations on pasta, sushi, salads, fresh fillets of grilled meat and fish with fruity accompaniments, and amusingly named options such as 'The Ugly but Good Toadfish'. Inside is beachy, breezy and informal. Get a table outside on the atmospheric decking and join the micro-celebs and a local crowd of young professionals. You might not expect to be California dreaming in Rome, but for the curious it's a fun night out and worth the trek for something a little different.

Food 8, Service 8, Atmosphere 8

Enoteca Ferrara, Via del Moro 1A, Trastevere
Tel: 06 583 3920   www.enotecaferrara.it
Open: 7.30–11.30pm daily.   €70
Italian

Hailed as one of the finest gastronomic experiences in Rome, Ferrara has all the trappings of a pretentious, arrogant eaterie, with its formal layout and starched white tablecloths, and service that is characteristically not of the

calibre the pretensions aspire to. But when it comes to wine, sisters and owners Lina and Maria certainly know their stuff. Enoteca Ferrara is winner of Best Enoteca in Italy in 2003, and vinophiles will adore the encyclopaedic selection of international wines, served in six specially designed types of glass. Perhaps the food takes second place because they are such slaves to the ambrosial grape. Consider going for dinner here as an expensive way of lining your stomach while experiencing some shamanistic wine enlightenment. You'd be better off enjoying a lip-smacking meal in a down-at-heel *trattoria* for half the price if your stomach is pining for pasta.

Food 6, Service 7, Atmosphere 7

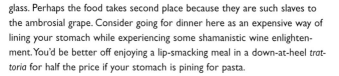

F.I.S.H., Via dei Serpenti 16, Centro Storico
Tel: 06 4782 4962   www.f-i-s-h.it
Open: 7.30–11.30pm daily   €60
Seafood

On the charming Via dei Serpenti in the heart of the Monti district, F.I.S.H. (Fine International Seafood House) is a fashionable staple for the down-to-earth glitterati who frequent this part of town. A fairly clubby atmosphere

permeates the three small rooms that offer first of all, out front on raised tables around the bar, *aperitivo* and snacks; a sushi bar in the next room; and then an intimate dining or 'grill room' at the back. Book ahead and get a table rather than perching at the rather anonymous sushi bar. As the name suggests, the menu is dominated by aquatic offerings, all with an Asian flavour, but if you do still want to go native there are plenty of departures. Service is very helpful, but the sushi could have been a little more chilled (likewise the sake).

Food 7, Service 8, Atmosphere 7

Glass Hostaria, Vicolo del Cinque 58, Trastevere

Tel: 06 5833 5903   www.glass-hostaria.it

Open: 8pm–2am daily   €50

Modern Italian

Part of the new generation of Roman restaurants, Glass Hostaria is a slice of civilized and contemporary restaurant dining in among the rowdy Trastevere tourist traffic. In an attempt to 'give Trastevere back to the Romans', dishes are modern and fresh interpretations of Italian cuisine, but some 'variations' can be a little unexpected. Portions are fairly small and

there are no side dishes, so don't come here if you're yearning for a steaming bowl of pasta and a slab of meat. However, for an invigorating gourmet experience, especially in the summer months when lighter, more delicate flavours are what you want, this is a stylish choice. The interior design follows the template for 'modern' restaurants, with glass floors and high-tech lighting. And for a restaurant this epicurean, the prices really are remarkably economical. Service is young, quick and friendly and the atmosphere is relaxed.

Food 8, Service 7, Atmosphere 7

Gusto, Piazza Augusto Imperatore 9, Centro Storico

Tel: 06 322 6273   www.gusto.it

Open: noon–3pm, 7.30pm–midnight daily; pizzeria 8pm–1am daily; wine bar 10am–2am daily   Restaurant: €50; Pizzeria: €20

Fusion

A multi-tasking, schizophrenic establishment by the mausoleum of Augustus, Gusto can't decide whether it's a wine bar, restaurant, bookshop or pizzeria. It is in fact all of the above (split-level), and moreover holds the mantle as grandfather of the new breed of Roman dining. The wine bar at the back is well suited to clandestine meetings and has a convivial air. Wines are served by the glass, alongside nibbles of cheese and meats in the stylish, brasserie-like setting. Upstairs the restaurant is a little more pretentious, attempting an Italian–Asian fusion with varying degrees of success. Weekend brunch is a riotous affair, with a vulture-like scrum over the delicious buffet. Arrive early to avoid disappointment, and remember you pay by the weight of food which, you'll find when you reach the scales, can be quite alarming. It may be getting long in the tooth by contemporary standards, but Gusto shows no sign of stopping – and the gang have recently opened a new venture in the same square, Osteria della Frezza, serving up traditional Roman cuisine but in a *tapas* style. This works well for those whose eyes are bigger than their *pancia,* which in Italy, is a rather common affliction.

Food 8, Service 7, Atmosphere 8

Hostaria dell'Orso, Via dei Soldati 25c, Centro Storico
Tel: 06 6830 1192   www.hdo.it
Open: 8pm–midnight. Closed Sundays and August.   €80
Italian

Once an inn accommodating the likes of Dante and then Goethe, Hostaria dell'Orso is housed in a 15th-century patrician *palazzo* on the banks of the Tiber. Enter through the atrociously cheesy piano bar and shimmy up the stairs to a rather formal restaurant that's under the command of Milanese super-chef Gualtiero Marchesi. Although the staff are a touch supercilious, the orange leather seats and some conspicuous modern art seek to lighten the load a little. The food, however, speaks for itself and certainly reaches

the mark of the prices. Try and secure a table on the *loggia* for romantic views, and if you fancy a bounce after dinner there's popular nightclub La Cabala just upstairs.

Food 8, Service 8, Atmosphere 8

Hosteria del Pesce, Via di Monserrato 25c, Centro Storico
Tel: 06 686 5617
Open: 7–11.30pm. Closed Sundays.   €80
Seafood

Acutely fashionable and glamorous, despite being, by all accounts, a massively overpriced fish restaurant. Come face to face with your crustacean friends at the entrance and then proceed inside to the snug restaurant with low

lighting and wooden tables for a menu that is strictly surf rather than turf. Everyone in here thinks that they're a star, but the almost surgical inspection lights hang over the tables shining on the real star of the show,

which is the simple, well-executed seafood, fresh daily from nearby Terracina. The seating is intimate, verging on cramped (and the clientele rather snooty), but at least you know that you're in the hottest restaurant in Rome. One glimpse at the champagne list and you get an idea of what to expect. Thank goodness those €800 bottles of Krug are on hand for special occasions when *prosecco* simply won't do. With prices this steep, take your time and linger till late – staff are friendly and enthusiastic with *digestivi*, so get stuck into a grappa or two and tell everyone that you're on TV back home.

Food 8, Service 7, Atmosphere 8

Maccheroni, Piazza delle Coppelle 44, Centro Storico
Tel: 06 6830 7895   www.ristorantemaccheroni.com
Open: 1–3pm, 8pm–midnight daily   €40
Italian

A reliable Centro Storico staple with simple, well-executed and traditional Roman cuisine. In summer, tables spill out onto the cobbles and diners are privy to the razzmatazz of the nearby bars. Actors, journalists, politicians and intelligentsia mingle with a low-key fashion set. Make sure you get a table

upstairs in the *sala sopra*, since below seems to have some problems with damp. Cool artwork lines the whitewashed walls, but the rest of the décor is strictly old-school, with wooden tables and chairs. Glimpse into the frenetic kitchen and see satisfying pasta dishes and lip-smacking meats emerge. Be sure not to rush over dinner, as it's a bustly, clubby atmosphere

– *molto* fun and a perfect warm-up supper for a night of hedonistic capers around the Piazza Navona drinking triangle.

Food 8, Service 7, Atmosphere 9

Il Margutta Ristoante, Via Margutta 118, Centro Storico
Tel: 06 3265 0577   www.ilmargutta.it
Open: 12.30–3.30pm, 7.30–11.30pm daily   €60
Vegetarian

This restaurant has been serving a fully vegetarian menu since its inception in 1979, which may account for the rather odd elevator-style background music. Seemingly a little too large for its own good, the interior is nevertheless pleasantly decorated with exuberant pieces of art adorning the walls. An extravagant wine list, excellent service and an ample cheeseboard make for a pleasing experience overall. *Dolce* are gratifyingly delicious, so those

with food issues can begin by feeling comfortably virtuous and then gravitate towards self-loathing with a cholesterol-laden end to their meal. Equally, for those visitors to Rome who are struggling to maintain their vegan or macrobiotic diet, this would be a godsend.

Food 8, Service 7, Atmosphere 7

Mezzo, Via di Priscilla 25/a, Rome

Tel: 06 8639 9017
Open: 8pm–midnight. Closed Sundays. €50
Italian

Mezzo is a slinky, stylish, New York-style eaterie with white walls and high
ceilings. Apparently inspired by London's restaurant of the same name, in
reality it bears very little resemblance to the English Mezzo. First, because
the food is actually rather fantastic, ranging from wood-fired pizza to tasty
grilled meats in generous portions, which you wouldn't expect from the
average waistline of the clientele. Like most places in the '*alta borghese*'
Parioli district, waitresses look like part-time models or actresses, as do

many of the diners. Dress up, preferably in tight white jeans or chinos, and
you'll fit in a treat. When it's busy, the kitchen is fairly slow, but the food is
worth the wait and the atmosphere distracting enough for you not to
notice. In the warmer months outside tables under the vines add to the all-
round aesthetic appeal. Youthful and modish, but with a convincing generation span of cool cats.

Food 8, Service 7, Atmosphere 8

Il Pagliaccio, Via dei Banchi Vecchi 129a, Centro Storico

Tel: 06 688 09595 www.ristoranteilpagliaccio.it
Open: 1–2.30pm, 8–10.30pm. Closed Monday lunch and Sundays. €80
Mediterranean fusion

An exceptional restaurant on almost all counts, where Michelin-starred chef Anthony Genovese has been captivating contemporary Romans with his

Mediterranean concoctions tinged with Asiatic touches for two years. You won't find *ossobuco alla romana* or *bucatini all'amatriciana* here, but you will find delicate flavours and interesting departures from the classical Roman menu, while acclaimed pastry chef Marion Lichtle rounds off the meal with choice desserts. Whereas some creative cuisine can be rather challenging, Genovese's offerings are still accessible even to the non-gourmet palate. However, prohibitive prices have made this a haunt for businessmen and culinary connoisseurs, creating rather rarefied atmosphere that comple- ments the white tablecloths and plush baroque upholstery. Some of the comments on the menu ('Tradition out of my heart tasting menu') may seem a little sentimental to the cynic's eye but all is forgiven on account of the excellent service (with impeccable English) and impressive food.

Food 9, Service 9, Atmosphere 8

Palatium, Via Frattina 94, Via Veneto
Tel: 06 6920 2132
Open: 1–3pm, 6–midnight. Closed Sundays. €40
Italian – Lazian

This modern restaurant and *enoteca* is dedicated to cuisine from the oft- forgotten region of Lazio. The name refers to the Palatine, one of the seven hills of Rome, but it's in fact nearer to the Spanish Steps and shopping-land than to the Palatine. Inside is a tranquil space with a fresh, invigorating layout and modern high-tech finishings. The focus is on promoting regional food and wine: diners sit on cubic chairs at polished wooden tables for a swig of something local accompanied by some cheese and cured meats, or alternatively eat properly in the minimalist dining room upstairs. The location is a little soulless come eveningtime when the shoppers have gone

home, but food hits the spot and there are plenty of light and healthy options – this is modern Lazio cuisine, as opposed to tripe and oxtail.

Food 8, Service 8, Atmosphere 7

Pierluigi, Piazza dei Ricci 144, Centro Storico
Tel: 06 686 8717 www.pierluigi.it
Open: 7.30–11.30pm. Closed Tuesdays.   €50
Seafood

Pierluigi caters to the dreams of those seeking a picture-postcard Roman holiday, and indeed everyone seems to have a soft spot for this dependable restaurant. The pretty 16th-century piazza is strewn with tables with a rather grown-up crowd (lots of foreign ex-pats and elegant Italians). Delicious and sizable portions of meat, fish and traditional Roman *primi piatti* are on offer, but the choice and quality of *dolce* leaves a little to be desired. Seafood is the star of the show here, displayed on an abundant flourish of ice. Inside the monochrome yellow walls are a little austere, but outside is decidedly more atmospheric, surrounded by artisan woodcutters' shops and crumbling *palazzi*..

Food 8, Service 7, Atmosphere 7

Pizzeria Montecarlo, Vicolo Savelli 13, Centro Storico

Tel: 06 686 1877 www.sevoinapizzadillo.com
Open: 6.30pm–midnight daily   €18
Italian – Pizza

Along with Da Baffetto around the corner, and Da Francesco in Piazza del
Fico, this rustic pizzeria is the third in the great pizza triumvirate around
Piazza Navona. The draw here is the fantastic *fritti* (deep-fried courgette
flowers oozing hot mozzarella), or the *suppli* (fried risotto balls stuffed with
ragu or cheese). Pizza is of course thin and crispy *alla romana* and unequivocally delicious, to be consumed at the plastic garden tables slung outside on

the shady *vicolo*. Service can be surly and brusque and you almost always have to wait for a table (especially in winter when there are fewer of them), but persevere and enjoy the traffic of Roman eccentrics. Cheap, cheerful and chaotic, it seems always to be open for a late-night feed, while lovers linger in clinches in the street outside.

Food 8, Service 7, Atmosphere 8

Pommidoro, Piazza dei Sanniti 44, San Lorenzo

Tel: 06 445 2692

Open: 12.30–3.30pm, 7.30–11.30pm. Closed Mondays. €40

Italian

A carnivorous choice of restaurant which pulses with proleteriat chic. Pommidoro is like the mothership of San Lorenzo and was famously adored by left-wing writer and film-maker Pier Paolo Pasolini. Settle in for a rustic meal by the fireplace in the interior dining room, or take a seat on the veranda in the piazza outside. Meat – especially game – is the speciality here, with an award-winning *spaghetti carbonara* and other hearty '*populus romanus*' fodder. If in doubt do as the old gents do and order a *bistecca* and swallow it down with a dousing of *vino rosso*. Visceral, brash and reassuringly authentic.

Food 8, Service 6, Atmosphere 8

La Rosetta, Via della Rosetta 9, Centro Storico

Tel: 06 686 1002

Open: 1–3pm, 7–11.30pm daily. Closed Sundays and August. €80

Seafood

Massimo Riccioli's lauded fish restaurant feels like a ship inside, all wooden portholes and white tablecloths, and the most comprehensive list of Mediterranean aquatic creatures imaginable. In business since 1966, the twinkly-eyed Massimo is now known as the seafood 'guru' of Rome. Prices may be astronomical but quality and presentation are faultless, while service is exemplary without being snooty, and wine aficionados will delight at the extensive list of French and Italian wines. Lunch is a more affordable option for the impecunious, with an excellent *degustazione* (tasting) menu. The

atmosphere is formal and rarefied, with lots of rich American Grand Tourists, businessmen and personal friends of Massimo who – of course, darling! – order off menu. Try not to miss the home-made desserts, or the fish soup.

Food 9, Service 9, Atmosphere 8

Santa Lucia, Largo Febo 12, Centro Storico
Tel: 06 6880 2427 www.santalucia-bartolo.com
Open: 7.30pm–midnight. Closed Tuesdays.   €60
Mediterranean

Some people think it's hard to find a decent restaurant around the hellishly touristy Piazza Navona, but these complainants have forgotten how to use their discerning eyes. Santa Lucia is a prime example of an excellent restaurant spitting-distance from the square, yet a world away from the caricature cartoon artists and tacky tat. Presided over by Bartolo Cuomo, the Neapolitan grand-daddy of Roman nightlife, this restaurant is the definition of contemporary Roman glamour, with a dark wood interior and a fine collection of paintings and drawings by contemporary artists. The food is a feast of modern Mediterranean classics with a leaning towards flavours from the Amalfi Coast, and has lined the stomachs of everyone from Bill

Clinton to Sophia Loren. Despite the accolade of these lofty diners the atmosphere is very down-to-earth, and prices are far from extortionate. Cosy up in the sexy interior, or sit under the trees in the courtyard festooned with fairy-lights. Really, really cool.

Food 8, Service 8, Atmosphere 8

Il Simposio di Costantini, Piazza Cavour 16, Prati
Tel: 06 321 3210
Open: noon–11pm Mon-Fri; 6-11pm Sat   €70
Italian

This rather stuffy wine bar and restaurant on Piazza Cavour is very appealing in the colder months, when you can neck back some corpulent wines in a sumptuous interior of wooden panels, velvet curtains and wrought-iron vines. Food is a fittingly fanciful affair, with marinated and

smoked fish tinged with a traditional Roman touch. Il Simposio is a grown-up and classy choice; and, if it's your wont, lunchtime is the right moment to snare a rich Italian magnate while he's polishing off an 80-strong cheese-board in the mirrored dining room.

Food 8, Service 8, Atmosphere 7

Taverna Angelica, Piazza A. Capponi 6, Borgo Pio
Tel: 06 687 4514 www.tavernanangelica.it
Open: 12.30–2.30pm, 7.30–11.30pm. Closed Sunday lunch.   €50
Italian

This is a decent choice in the lost corner of Borgo Pio – an area that predominantly caters to the touristy backwash of Vatican visitors with unconvincing cuisine. The food is very good; it's clean, healthy and flavour-some, with modern recipes of meat and fish which resist any pretensions.

The Sunday lunch set menu is particularly appealing after a visit to see the Big Daddy himself round the corner. But they haven't quite got it right in terms of styling – inside looks a bit like an Oriental restaurant, with wicker Vietnamese-style lampshades – but, God bless them, they're really trying to pull the area out of its bland culinary quagmire, over 400 wines and a hand-some selection of cheeses really make the grade. Despite the slightly cold atmosphere you may find yourself chowing down alongside a cassocked priest or two slugging back the *vino rosso* on a break from the Hail Marys.

Food 7, Service 8, Atmosphere 6

La Taverna Degli Amici, Piazza Margana, 36, Centro Storico

Tel: 06 6992 0637

Open: 1–3pm, 7.30–11pm. Closed Monday lunch. €60

Italian - Roman

This heavenly refuge sits in the corner of an ivy-clad square behind the traffic hub of Piazza Venezia and just begs summertime lunchtime boozing. The menu is ample without being overwhelming, and the food, which is subtly priced, is exceptionally good: classic Roman dishes such as *tonarelli cacio e pepe* and plenty of

grilled meat and fish choices. *Antipasti* include a delectably juicy buffalo mozzarella and *prosciutto*. An outside table in the leafy square is where you want to be, sitting with a glass of wine while you observe the romantic traffic of behind-the-scenes Rome. Perfectly situated for a post-prandial wan-

der through the backstreets of the ghetto, and perhaps, if you fancy popping into the church of Santa Maria Campitelli, a sumptuous encounter with the baroque.

Food 8, Service 7, Atmosphere 8

La Terrazza, Hotel Eden, Via Ludovisi 49, Via Veneto

Tel: 06 478 121   www.hotel-eden.it

Open: 12.30–3.30pm, 7.30–11.30pm daily €130

Italian

Boasting possibly the most heart-pinchingly lovely view of Rome, the Michelin-starred La Terazza restaurant is on the top floor of the Hotel Eden. The 360-degree panorama of the Eternal City skyline is genuinely breathtaking, whether at lunchtime or when illuminated under a starry sky. Cuisine is also unequivocally excellent and suits a range of palates from the adventurous to the traditional, with creative classics from chef Adriano Cavagnini.

The house speciality is the *fiori di zucca* (courgette flowers), which we defy anyone not to enjoy. It's best to book a week in advance, but staff are very accommodating and may be able to offer a table on the terrifically lovely terrace, which smokers may prefer anyway. Romantic and traditionally glamorous without being staid, this makes for an unforgettable winner on an onerous occasion.

Food 9, Service 9, Atmosphere 8

Tiepolo, Via G.B Tiepolo 3–5, Roma Nord
Tel: 06 322 7449
Open: 12.30pm–2am daily   €30
International

A relaxed and funky choice in Roma Nord, Tiepolo is a tourist-free zone, populated by a young and fashionable crowd who've clearly made this bistro part of their scene. Inside is cosy and laid-back, with a smattering of tables on the pavement outside. The simple menu here is Scandinavian-influenced (including a range of stuffed baked potatoes), and features healthy daily specials which are tasty and satisfying (with the occasional quiche Lorraine). Cooking is honest and casual, but the buzzy atmosphere, fabulous desserts and healthy array of wines all under €20 make it well worth a trip for a relaxed meal off the beaten track.

Food 8, Service 7, Atmosphere 8

Tram Tram, Via dei Reti 44–46, San Lorenzo
Tel: 06 490 416
Open: 12.30–3.30pm, 7.30–11.30pm. Closed Mondays. €40
Italian – Puglian

Rooted in the bowels of San Lorenzo, Tram Tram was definitely born on the right side of the bohemian tracks. Behind the lace curtains Signora di

Vittorio serves Puglian-inspired dishes that have forged a faithful following of devotees from all over the city. Look on the walls for remnants salvaged from old trams, which give this *trattoria* its name. While service is not the most professional you'll find, the bustly atmosphere and satisfying spreads have secured Tram Tram's reputation as one of the coolest and most distinctive eateries in Rome.

Food 8, Service 8, Atmosphere 7

Trattoria, Via Pozzo delle Cornacchie 25, Centro Storico
Tel: 06 6830 1427 www.ristorantetrattoria.it
Open: 1–3pm, 7–11.30pm. Closed Sundays.   €60
Southern Italian and Sicilian

Star Italian architects the Giametta brothers have created an ultra-minimalist space for Sicilian chef Filippo La Mantia's fashionable restaurant. A former photo-journalist, the ebullient and charming Filippo reworks southern Italian and Sicilian classics with a lighter than light feel. This of course makes him extremely popular with a fashionable crowd who are constantly watching the pounds. With his culinary alchemy he has discovered a way to cook without onion or garlic, which by all accounts is impossible in Italian cuisine,

but a godsend to those with IBS. His signature *caponata* dish (a ratatouille of vegetables) is wonderful, as are the other dishes on the menu, often influenced heavily by Filippo's South-East Asian escapades. Some complain about the lack of windows in the restaurant, but with the beautifully presented dishes, gorgeous clientele and glass-walled kitchen where the maestro works his magic, there's plenty to look at inside. Service can be a little erratic, but the overall mood is courteous, friendly and intimate.

Food 8, Service 8, Atmosphere 8

Tutti Frutti, Via Luca della Robbia 3A, Testaccio

Tel: 06 575 7902
Open: 8pm–midnight daily   €35
Italian

A real hidden gem in rustic, authentic Testaccio, Tutti Frutti is an artsy,
informal and friendly dining spot. The hieroglyphic handwritten menu
requires some elucidation but once you decipher the daily specials with a

little help from owner Michele, you'll soon discover that the food is
splendid. Whereas most eateries in this part of town have traditional menus
of offal and tripe, the cuisine is fresh, contemporary and much less scary.
Behind the discreet frosted glass entrance you'll find an interior that's
spacious and basic, yet with some colourful touches. The kitchen is open till
late and so close to the club strip that you can bounce out of the door and
find yourself straight on the pulsing Via Galvani. It's as good for a quick bite
as it is for lingering over carafes of wine alongside a sophisticated, cultured
yet unostentatious set.

Food 8, Service 8, Atmosphere 8

Uno e Bino, Via degli Equi 58, San Lorenzo

Tel: 06 446 0702
Open: 7.30pm–midnight daily. Closed Mondays.   €70
Italian

A clean, chic and uncomplicated *enoteca* in the heart of Via degli Equi has a discrete, blink-and-you'll-miss-it entrance. Once you're inside, jazzy background music lets you know you're in the cool part of town. Being an *enoteca*, the focus is of course on wine, as laid-back owner Giampaolo Gravina guides diners through the ample list. The atmosphere is intimate, with a number of tables *à deux*, and it's rather tiny, so booking is recom-

mended. Perfectly cosy during the colder months, but those who prefer *al fresco* dining in the summer may like to go elsewhere. A *degustazione* (tasting) menu of four plates for €40 is excellent value, while Umbrian and Sicilian undertones characterize the *à la carte*, which is of a very high standard considering that this is technically a wine bar. Service is young, friendly and professional, in what is ultimately a relaxingly stylish environment.

Food 8, Service 8, Atmosphere 8

Vinarium, Via dei Volsci 107, San Lorenzo
Tel: 06 446 2110
Open: 8pm–1am. Closed Mondays. €60
Italian

A candle-lit temple to gastronomic adventures – sit down and strap yourself in for some sensory explosions. Run by young couple Elena and Enrico, this is a classy, well-managed venture that has the air of being a rather well-kept secret. An important selection of 900 wines are reassuringly presented and the lengthy menu oozes quality cooking that's a touch above the more rustic fare on offer in San Lorenzo. Late business hours accommodate the bohemian night owls under the vaulted ceilings and exposed brick walls.

Refined, classic and intimate, it's popular with local artists from the studios in the nearby Cerere, a former pasta factory.

Food 8, Service 8, Atmosphere 8

Vizi Capitali, Via della Renella 94, Trastevere

Tel: 06 581 8840 www.vizicapitali.com
Open: 7pm–midnight. Closed Sundays.   €50
Italian

Don't be put off by the incongruous-looking sign over the door, which gives you the impression that you're about to enter an Eighties steakhouse – this is a genuine find amid the rather mediocre Trastevere tourist *trattorie*. The restaurant's name translates as the 'seven deadly sins' and reflects owner Marco Scandola's self-confessed fascination both for human nature and for cooking. Characters from Dante's *Inferno* inspire the dishes on the menu

and two tasting menus are offered – for the 'proud' or for the 'gluttonous'. An interesting mix of clean flavours and scents suits the wooden furnished interior, but the décor is a little confused. White minimalist walls and chic wooden tables are accompanied by gold garlands and knick-knack pound-shop gold cherubs in a slightly jarring mix. But all can be forgiven for the culinary attention to detail, the well-executed and presented food and the gracious standard of service that overrides the prices. Regional wines from Lazio also make a convincing appearance on the 70-strong list. The atmosphere lacks stuffiness but still retains an elegance that makes it as suitable for an intimate, romantic meal as it does for an informal, pre-clubbing supper. Very popular.

Food 8, Service 8, Atmosphere 8

Zen Sushi, Via degli Scipioni 243, Prati
Tel: 06 321 3420   www.zenworld.it
Open: 1–3pm, 8–11.30pm. Closed Saturday lunch and Mondays.   €45
Japanese

Now feeding fashion-conscious Romans for four years, this Roman outpost of Zen Sushi follows the format of the Milanese mothership. Lunchtime is a straightforward affair with plates of sushi, sashimi and tempura on a revolving carousel. Get there just before 1pm to secure a table alongside the ladies with neat ponytails and other harbingers of bourgeois style. Décor

feels a little James Bond, with a mix of contemporary art shows decorating the walls, and suits the crowd of sushi devotees that London and New York must have had in the 1980s. Consequently, you may be surprised to find quite a few pre-pubescents in evidence, dragged along by parents keen to sophisticate their brat-pack kids' palates. The sushi is really very good – at dinner time try the boat platter selection of fish brought on a wooden boat. All in all, the food is as accomplished as in any authentic Japanese restaurant, but as this is Italy, coffee is on hand to round off the meal in a decidedly un-oriental fashion. Italians, after all, just have to have it their way.

Food 8, Service 8, Atmosphere 8

Notes & Updates

Notes & Updates

drink...

All it takes is a little cultural retuning to log into Rome's eclectic drinking environment. The city has yet to fully assume a chic designer drinking scene in glamorous haunts, which is why most fun is to be had in the *aperitivo* bars that are popping up all over the capital, drinking *al fresco* outside cafés, or getting sozzled in wine bars.

Some of the newer cocktail bars can feel a little sterile and jar with the antique cityscape, so think twice before forgoing the traditional *enoteca* (where you can sample cold meats and cheeses with your wine) in favour of the glitzy new temple to lychee Martinis. On the rise is the hotel bar scene, with glamorous rooftops to sup on a sundowner in style; try the Radisson SAS, Hotel 47 at the foot of the Capitoline hill, or for a seriously romantic *prosecco* at dusk, the Hotel Eden.

Of late there is a growing trend for bookshop-wine bars, which attract the young and fashionable intelligentsia in the bohemian quarters of the city. These are interesting and unexpected modish hotspots, notably Bar a Book in San Lorenzo and Libreria del Cinema in Trastevere.

Be warned (or delighted) that measures of alcohol are typically Mediterranean, hence the tendency to skip dinner once your hunger magically disappears after two negronis. But the hegemony of food in Italy means that you rarely drink without nibbling at the same time, which is why you'll see few incidents of obscene inebriation in Rome. At least in these stakes, Italians do it better.

The ubiquitous northern Italian ritual of *aperitivo* is taking over the city's bars. This extremely civilized practice involves spreads of tantalizing snacks laid out in the early evening in many bars for you to graze on free of charge (the cost is actually swallowed up in the price of your drink). The most abundant and buzzy are Freni e Frizioni and Societe Lutece.

The Romans like two types of pre-dinner cocktail, the negroni (Campari, Martini Rosso and a mind-bending wallop of gin) and, in the summer months, the mojito. The best (and strongest) can be found at what are perhaps the coolest cocktail hotspots *du jour*, again Societe Lutece and Freni e Frizioni. Strawberry caipirinhas are also recently all the rage.

The other option is to settle down in an *enoteca* – a wine bar where plates of *salumi e formaggi* (cold cuts of meats like salami, *prosciutto*, *bresaola* and

deliciously smelly cheeses) are served with wines by the bottle or the glass. Heavenly, especially in the colder months. Try Al Vino al Vino in Monti or Il Goccetto in Centro Storico.

There is a certain staple *circus maximus* of Roman bars, which for the most part resemble cafés and provide you with a place

to sit down and watch the *dolce vita* traffic pass by in all its various forms. These lie on the well-trodden haunt behind Piazza Navona, but are not always easy to find – which is exactly what makes them special. Look for Bar del Fico, Giulio Passami Olio and Bar della Pace.

The Romans are lazy – they like to take a load off and have a chat. Once you get this right, you'll have an MSc in *caput mundi* boozing.

Be aware of the somewhat frustrating 'cassa' system – don't even think about joining the crush at the bar before you get your *scontrino* (drinks ticket) from the till. It means you have to queue twice, but when in Rome…

7th Heaven Bar, Aleph Hotel, Via San Basilio 15, Centro Storico
Tel: 06 422 901
Open: 10am–2am daily

On a balmy summer evening, there are few sexier places to sup a clandestine cocktail than the roof terrace of the Aleph Hotel. Since the Romans haven't taken naturally to drinking in hotel bars, 7th Heaven, with its seduc-

tive white marshmallow chairs and exotic flowers on candle-lit decking, still feels like a well-kept secret. Don't miss the retro neon Martini sign glowing in the distance amid the sprawl of Roman rooftops. Early in the week, lonely businessmen dine with their mobile phones, but things warm up later on when a fashion crowd descends to party. Service is a little slow, but the location and intimacy more than justifies the sacrifice. Get yourself in the mood in the sexy lift, emblazoned with paparazzi images from past *dolce vita* dreams.

Al Vino al Vino, Via dei Serpenti 19, Monti
Tel: 06 485 803
Open: 6pm–midnight daily

Known affectionately as 'Da Luca' by the arty Monti residents who treat this little *enoteca* like their own living room, it takes its adopted moniker from the ebullient, if a little dipsomaniac, Luca, who runs the place seemingly haphazardly, but to great success. This is a grown-up yet lively local institution, ever popular and serving wines by the bottle and glass with great plates of

cheese and ham carved up from behind the small bar, and light meals if you just can't be bothered to move. (This is likely to happen once you settle in.) Turn up early evening and you're bound to make friends with all and sundry, picking up a spot of local gossip along the way as well. The bar itself is an old pharmacy – small, cosy and authentic and still supplying a tonic of sorts. The only potential problem is that it lacks any outside seating, but the low-key atmosphere is one of the most charming in Rome. You'll be smitten.

Antico Caffè della Pace, Via della Pace 37, Centro Storico
Tel: 06 686 1216
Open: 9am–2am. Closed Monday mornings.

Bar della Pace (as it's colloquially known) has always been earmarked as one of Rome's *dolce vita* hotspots, where the beautiful people go to see and be

seen. The true zeitgeist trendoids have moved on (just round the corner to Societe Lutece), but the media crowd have adopted the Art Deco-style room with its white marble tables as their office. This place is all about location – it enjoys a favoured position under a cascade of ivy on one of Rome's most beautiful streets, in the shadow of the baroque church of Santa Maria della Pace. Given its decidedly romantic atmosphere, it's as good for a morning cappuccino or a pre-prandial *prosecco* as it is for late night navel-gazing.

Aqua Negra, Largo del Teatro Valle 9, Centro Storico
Tel: 06 9760 6026
Open: 11am–2am daily

Although predominately a restaurant, this glass box behind the Teatro della Valle drums up more of a crowd for drinks than for dinner. An elegant and sexy Italian crowd descends on this fairly new spot, which comes alive at

aperitivo hour, especially mid-week. The location favours those who work nearby, and design is coolly contemporary with flickering candlelight and coloured glass. The cocktail list is ample with some inspired touches in the form of daiquiris and mandarin and lychee Martinis. If you want to blend in, wear this season's Armani, in black of course, and don't forget your shades.

Arco degli Aurunci, Via degli Aurunci 42, San Lorenzo
Tel: 06 445 4425
Open: 9am–1am daily

Set in San Lorenzo's epicentre, this is a good spot for pre- or post-prandial drinking. Perched on the corner of the neighbourhood's main square, it offers unrivalled ringside seating from where you can enjoy the ebb and flow of bohemian traffic. Inside it is modern and unpretentious, and it is a little reminiscent of a college campus — which comes as no surprise since Rome's biggest university is just around the corner. If you're in the area

for dinner it's worth stopping by for a cocktail, if only to watch the action in the square where lots of bespectacled, skinny cuties flock to swap stories and share those interestingly scented cigarettes. Thursday nights are enlivened with live jazz after dinner.

Bar a Book, Via dei Piceni 23, San Lorenzo
Tel: 06 4544 5438
Open: 10am–10pm. Closed Mondays.

A quirky and happening spot on the edge of the arty San Lorenzo area that comfortably marries the intellectual rigours of books and booze. Bar a Book

is one of the first of its kind in the capital's burgeoning trend for such convivial spots. Get lost in the kaleidoscopic shelves of colourful art, literature and photography books with no pressure to buy, or pull up a pew at the central table amid all the retro design décor and peruse the newspapers round the clock with a laidback, cool and clever crowd. The day starts with a cappuccino and croissant and continues via lunch snacks to a pre-supper *aperitivo* and then relaxed de-parching and discussion after dark. Perfect for a glass of wine and some book shopping before dinner at the nearby Tram Tram restaurant.

Bar del Fico, Piazza del Fico 26, Centro Storico
Tel: 06 686 5205
Open: 9am–2am. Closed Sunday mornings.

A perennial favourite, Bar del Fico sits behind the late-night detritus of the now rather tacky Piazza Navona and attracts a consistently cool crowd of revellers who gather under the canopy of the bedecked fig tree supping

cocktails 'til the wee hours. A dairy in a former life, this bar gives the impression that it's been here forever, taking its name from the fig tree that emerges unapologetically from the foundations of the building. The bar, run by a convivial crowd, enjoys a certain transition throughout the day – septuagenarians banter in the shade and play chess well into the afternoon before Romans and *cognoscenti* foreigners take over the nocturnal shift. An essential Roman experience.

Bar San Calisto, Piazza San Calisto 4, Trastevere

Tel: 06 583 5869

Open: 8am–2am. Closed Sundays and end of August.

A veritable Trastevere institution, this bar is a meeting-point and melting-pot of local characters, out-of-work actors and fun-loving criminals. San Calisto may be cheap as chips and a little down-at-heel, but you can't help but love

it. Just don't expect too much finesse. There's an original 1950s interior, football posters from the last century and lighting that would make even Sophia Loren look a little wan. Stop for coffee or ice cream during the day, or while away the evening sitting outside with a motley crew ranging from the young and beautiful to the slightly rough around the edges (so don't be surprised if things end up getting quite chatty). Try a *sgroppino* (a lemon sorbet doused in vodka), an *affogato* (ice cream literally 'drowned' in liquor) or the chocolate ice cream – unofficially heralded as the best in the city. The bar staff are friendly, rowdy and really rather bonkers, but make friends with them at your peril – your servings of alcohol will be unbearably strong.

Café Riccioli, Piazza delle Coppelle 10A, Centro Storico

Tel: 06 6821 0313

Open: noon–2am daily

An offshoot of Massimo Riccioli's La Rosetta seafood restaurant, Café Riccioli serves excellent negronis and cocktails and a handsome *aperitivo* buffet, including sushi and healthy fresh fare to whet your appetite. This is a more contemporary and trendy little sister to the hallowed, grown-up La

Rosetta, bedecked in bright colours and with contemporary art donning the walls. *Aperitivo* and after-dinner drinks are buzzy and upbeat, and for those in need of an aphrodisiac (unlikely in one of the world's most romantic metropolis)

oysters and *prosecco* are on hand to kick-start your amorous metabolism. The menu of raw fish and light meals make this a model magnet, and the outside seating in the square is a delight in summer months.

Crudo, Via degli Specchi 6, Centro Storico
Tel: 06 683 8989
Open: 7.30pm–2am. Closed Sundays.

For those craving an alternative to the carb-fest of Italian cuisine, Crudo may be a welcome respite. Taking its name from the Italian word for 'raw', it specializes in just that, but its appeal lies more in the litany of drinks that would quench even the most parched palate. And its location, tucked away behind Largo Arenula, makes it feel like a private club, despite being very much in the thick of things around Campo dei Fiori. *Barbarella*-style leather chairs and projected images define the décor as strictly *nouveau Roma*. The well-stocked bar has a selection of draught beers and a line-up of well-mixed cocktails to rival any London establishment, with exceptionally fine vodka Martinis for those moments

when nothing else will do. Stay downstairs in the lounge and snack on sushi and *carpaccio* with Mediterranean hams and cheeses. And seeing as this is Japanese with an Italo twist, there's always a bread-basket to soak up the sake or that one Martini too many. Music is loungey (if a little formulaic), suiting the unpretentious crowd. Don't neglect the abundant selection of dessert wines, and enjoy the often rare sensation of finishing a meal in Italy without needing a forklift truck to cantilever you from your seat.

Freni e Frizioni, Via del Politeama 4–6, Trastevere
Tel: 06 5833 4210
Open: 10am–2am daily

The younger, rowdier sister bar to Societe Lutece has found a home in an old garage perched on the Lungotevere just by Ponte Sisto. It's great all day long for a breakfast cappuccino or light lunch, but it comes into its own with unencumbered hedonistic boozing every night of the week. Regular art shows from contemporary artists line the walls, complementing the ramshackle furniture and even more rambunctious revellers. As at Societe Lutece, a buffet of healthy delights is served up every evening from around 7 'til 10, when the price of a wine/beer or cocktail will be marked up to

include free gorging. Take note that it gets very busy, so it's not advisable if you get claustrophobic in crowds. Be warned also that measures can be eye-wateringly strong, and admittedly the *baristi* can be a little limited in expertise. To stay on the safe side go for a mojito or caipirinha, all of which will have you weak at the knees – that is, if your heart isn't already melting from the sight of all the young beauties cavorting in the square.

Galleria Santa Cecilia, Piazza di Santa Cecilia 16, Trastevere

Tel: 06 5833 4365 www.galleriasantacecilia.com
Open: 11am–midnight daily

This is another popular, minimalist bookshop and wine bar of the style that's infesting Roman drinking haunts of late. Set on the sophisticated side of Trastevere, opposite the church of Santa Cecilia, this watering-hole is attached to an acclaimed photography gallery run by Maria Evangelisti.

Bounteously stocked with photography and contemporary art books, the place comes alive in the evening, especially when a new show is festooned across the whitewashed walls. Get a fix of arty modernity over a glass of wine, see and be seen in the cube-like gallery bar and leaf through some photography tomes before plunging back into the rustic Roman ways with a hearty plate of *spaghetti all'amatriciana* in nearby Da Enzo trattoria.

Giulio Passami Olio, Via di Monte Giordano 28, Centro Storico

Tel: 06 6880 3288 www.giuliopassamiolio.it
Open: 10am–11.30pm daily

A veritable institution in the golden triangle of hotspots behind the detritus of tourism around Piazza Navona. Smell the scent of louche-drinking, clandestine encounters and *in vino veritas* as soon as you walk through the door. Giulio Passami Olio ('Pass the Oil, Giulio') has the look of a cosy taverna inside, with 1920s and '30s paraphernalia, wooden panels, barrels

and suggestive mirrors. Peaceful and sophisticated, this place effortlessly combines the air of authentic *enoteca* with a relaxed and sexy crowd that make the place their own till late into the evening.

Il Goccetto, Via dei Banchi Vecchi 14, Centro Storico

Tel: 06 686 4268

Open: 11.30am–2.30pm, 6–11pm. Closed Sundays, 1st week in Jan and 3 weeks in August.

Under a discreet sign saying nothing more than '*vini e oli*' ('oil and wine') lurks an authentic Roman wine bar in a medieval bishop's house amid the crumbling *palazzi* on the lovely Via dei Banchi Vecchi. A religious attitude remains, perhaps from its former occupant, but now with devotions fixed firmly on the wine rather than anything more holy. As welcome to the serious buff as to those looking for a quick swig before supper, Il Goccetto

has an atmospheric, slightly French feel, with wooden barrels, original beams and gothic-looking lanterns. Seating is casual, with a few scattered tables on the inside among the shelves of bottles, while locals and smokers linger on the steps outside. Plates of cold cuts of meats and cheeses are on offer to accompany your evening tipple and the vibe is relaxing, mellow and somewhat contemplative, suiting its grown-up clientele.

H Club Doney, Via Veneto 142, Via Veneto
Tel: 06 4708 2805
Open: 8am–1am, daily

Although the Via Veneto has certainly outlived its former 1960s heyday, the lounge bar H Club Doney, next door to the Westin Excelsior, still manages to retain some credibility. The modern-day Marcello Mastroiannis are proba-

bly on the other side of the river in Trastevere but the DJs still turn the beat around with a surprisingly good toe-tapping selection of tunes to galvanize you through a few rounds of Martinis. Following the template of the Milanese outpost, the bar boasts chandeliers and glam-rock black leather and zebra furnishings as a backdrop for getting you elegantly wasted. The crowd can be slightly mixed – you'll find trendy Romans as well as some uncertain high-rolling tourist types from the hotel next door – but don't let that put you off. Thursday nights are the musical appointment not to miss, when international DJs regularly claim the decks.

Ice Club, Via Madonna dei Monti 15, Via Veneto
Tel: 06 9784 5582
Open: 6pm–2am daily

A very new arrival to the burgeoning bohemian scene in beautiful Monti, this will surely help Romans keep their cool when temperatures and humidity soar. This is the first venture from two cool 20-somethings Matteo and Daniele, so expect a hip and sexy young crowd. Enter from the sweaty,

dusty street behind the Forum and don an insulating cloak and mittens before proceeding into the −5° bar made from 40 tons of ice. It's hard to tell how far this one will ride, but the refreshing respite it offers in the summer months and the novelty of the venture will surely make this a popular pitstop.

Libreria del Cinema, Via Fienaroli 31/r, Trastevere

Tel: 06 581 7724 www.libreriadelcinema.roma.it
Open: 11am–9pm (midnight Fri–Sat). Closed Monday mornings.

One of the few bastions left in a neighbourhood that's being swallowed up by mass tourism, this bookshop/wine bar can be found on Trastevere's coolest and prettiest street. A group of friends got together in 2004 to initiate this place, which doubles up as a creative exhibition and meeting space while managing to be a

beautiful bookshop at the same time. The glitterati of the film world descend on this supremely down-to-earth hotspot whenever they're in town so don't be surprised to find directors and screenwriters littering the pavement outside and plotting their next big thing over a cold glass of *passito*. Regular meetings and events mean it's always swarming with alluring intellectuals, who make a stunning contrast to the crusties bumming coins for cider round the corner.

Ombre Rosse, Piazza Sant'Egidio 12, Trastevere
Tel: 06 588 4155
Open: 8am (5pm Sun)–2am daily

Ombre Rosse will never be perennially cool or stylish, but it is reliable, the atmosphere is warm, the beer is cold and its location is without rival for whiling away a mellow evening in Trastevere. Since it's popular with foreign students and ex-pats, it's hard to secure a ringside table on the pretty patio outside (where it all gets very chatty and animated) until the wee hours. Inside is bedecked with black-and-white tiles and wooden tables, making it a cosy refuge in the colder months, especially for a light meal. Its location in the heart of Trastevere means that it's filled with a  menagerie from breakfast-time till last orders, sometimes with an impromptu spot of live music thrown into the mix. Perfect for a refreshing pint of beer or a lazy glass of wine with cheese without the obligatory *dolce vita* posing in other parts of town.

Rhome, Piazza Augusto Imperatore 46, Centro Storico
Tel: 06 6830 1430
Open: 1pm–2am daily. Closed Monday evenings.

Fascinating for many reasons, first of all for the steady traffic of coiffed, Cavalli-clad, diamante-encrusted 'girlfriends' who populate this recently renovated restaurant cum DJ bar. Second, because it used to be a rather successful fish restaurant called Reef, which seemingly vanished overnight (and no one really wants to talk about it). Porsches and Ferraris litter the

street outside, while inside tanned, powerful-looking men in suits and cashmere jumpers talk shop and the girls dance to a series of high-octane tunes in exchange for their new D&G handbags. Interestingly, there is no drinks menu (prices are extortionate) but there is a designated space for smokers; both are vaguely illegal in Italy. Elementary powers of deduction, therefore, make one think that this gig is a 'family run' affair, which makes it even more (precariously) entertaining as a fly on the wall at the bar. Design is very 1980s Manhattan, with lots of chrome, black marble and visceral accents of red, with stylish and skin-soft furniture courtesy of Poltrona Frau.

Salotto 42, Piazza di Pietra 42, Centro Storico
Tel: 06 678 5804
Open: 10am–1.30am. Closed Sundays.

A relaxed, unpretentious bar just off Via del Corso in the atmospheric Piazza di Pietra. Apparently owned by a Swedish supermodel, it attracts a similarly pulchritudinous, Cosmo-sipping clientele who sip coffee and peruse magazines on film, fashion and art under the 19th-century Murano crystal chandelier. Vintage 1950s furniture seats chic *derrieres*, and in the evening a

sophisticated cocktail crowd of scantily clad models descend, who snack on small *tapas*-style Swedish dishes as the soundtrack turns up. The menu includes a chocolate fondue, but you'll never see the Italians indulge in anything quite so compromising.

Shaki, Via del Governo Vecchio 123, Centro Storico
Tel: 06 683 08796
Open: 10am–midnight daily

Shaki sits on one of the premium corners for quaffing and people-watching day or night on the gorgeous Via del Governo Vecchio. Lunchtime sees style mavens nibbling on satisfying salads, while come early evening in the warmer

months, the outside tables fill with lovely-looking people drinking from the extensive tea and wine menu. The design just screams 'Milano', with coolly modern Japanese-inspired furnishings and curvy 1970s lounge shapes downstairs. A fine spot for *aperitivo* after a retail blitz along the funky Via del Governo Vecchio, or for a calmly chic sundowner before dinner around Piazza Navona. Thankfully the area has been newly pedestrianized, which has stopped the irritating roar of passing *motorini*.

Societe Lutece, Piazza Montevecchio 17, Centro Storico
Tel: 06 6830 1472
Open: 9am–2am daily

Rome's first injection of Northern Italian cool (the Romans are known to remain tenaciously provincial in their tastes) touched down three years in the hidden, hip area behind Santa Maria della Pace. This came as a delight to the beautiful people who have since abandoned their former stomping ground in Campo dei Fiori to the clutches of drunk tourists. Societe Lutece is small but perfectly formed, with some exceptionally attractive  bar staff, and at the weekends the battered record decks are taken full advantage of and the old schoolroom furniture takes a jostling. Scooters and car bonnets in the intimate square outside become temporary tables for resting potent cocktails – the Cuban mojito is the summer Roman classic. An abundant *aperitivo* buffet is served up daily around 7–10pm and includes pasta salads, rice dishes and raw vegetables (during which time the price of a drink will be slightly marked up). Be warned: a recent visit ended in cascades of water thrown from the windows of angry residents from the *palazzo* above, clearly sick of the rabble of bright young things drinking and flirting their way *ad alta voce* in the unfortunately acoustic square.

Stardust, Vicolo de' Renzi 4, Trastevere

Tel: 06 5832 0875

Open: 7pm–2am Mon–Sat; noon–2am Sun

A pocket-sized bar down a dark alley in Trastevere, often populated by long-haired, out-of-work actors and bearded pseudo-political incendiaries who slug cheap wine and discuss the merits of social anarchy. Don't let them intimidate you, though: inside is cosy and comfy. Here, the locals and the laidback styling will give you the feeling that you're at a cool, albeit small house party. Things shut late when the last (opinionated) reveller rolls out the door.

International and generous bar staff haphazardly choose the soundtrack from a kaleidoscopic selection ranging from reggae to the Eurythmics and whatever else is to hand.

Stravinskij Bar at Hotel de Russie, Via del Babuino 9, Centero Storico

Tel: 06 328 881

Open: 9am–1am daily

If you don't manage to rent a room alongside George and Brad in the timelessly glamorous Hotel de Russie, slip confidently into the bar for an early evening, or indeed early afternoon drink with the old-school divas, chuffed foreigners and the genteel *beau-monde* of Rome. The early evening piano

music may not be to everyone's taste but the setting is so fantastically civilized that it sort of escapes notice. Smugly satisfying, even if you are on your own and fancy reading the paper over a caviar Martini – let's face it, we all have those little moments on holiday. Service is discreet and impeccable and the recent addition of the butterfly oasis within the Renaissance-style gardens adds to the enchantment. Classic, irrefutable pleasure.

La Terrazza Bar at the Hotel Eden, Via Ludovisi 49, Via Veneto
Tel: 06 478 121 www.hotel-eden.it
Open: 10.30am–1am daily

If you don't manage a meal at the Michelin-starred Terrazza restaurant, at least pop up to the bar and fulfil any filmstar dreams you may be harbouring on your Roman holiday with a cocktail on the panoramic terrace at the Hotel Eden. Expect a rather formal collar-and-tie set, but then again, dressing up is so much fun, especially for this type of setting. Classic chic dominates the styling in the bar with cream-upholstered comfy chairs and low tables. The mood is similar to London's Claridge's, but with more English country house than Art Deco and a 360-degree view to die for. The signature house cocktail is the Sol Eden, a watermelon and vodka based

concoction, which is terminally refreshing. There are few things that could be more romantic than a sundown *prosecco* on the terrace with unrivalled views of *caput mundi*. Don't even think about coming here if you're mourning a lost romance – if there's anywhere that will get you in the mood for love, then this is the place.

Vineria Reggio, Campo dei Fiori 15, Centro Storico
Tel: 06 6880 3268
Open: 9am–1am. Closed Sundays during the day.

This wine bar is known affectionately by Romans simply as '*la vineria*', or 'the wine bar'. However, what was once the early evening meeting-spot for the sophisticated young Roman revellers who gave it their affectionate (or lazy)

nickname, has seen a bit of a decline of late due to the increasing squalor of Campo dei Fiori, one of Rome's oldest food and flower markets (unfortunately it now becomes a swarming mass of drunk young Americans after dark). That said, the exceptionally lively atmosphere and wine list make it worth a visit if you're passing. The mammoth selection of *vino* is served from the long bar while a few wooden benches line the cramped interior – this makes seating at a premium, and stilettos impractical. Standing at the bar means prices for a quick snifter of wine start at €1.50, making it a welcome pitstop on the evening itinerary. If you can, nab one of the outside tables and sit under the stern gaze of the statue of Giordano Bruno, the 16th-century philosopher who was burned at the stake.

Zest at Radisson SAS, Via Filippo Turati 171, Monti
Tel: 06 444 841   www.radissonsas.com
Open: 10am–1.30am daily

Another of Rome's finest rooftops, this place positively screams Miami/New Hamptons glamour with its azure swimming pool and curvy, Modernist architecture. Somewhat surprisingly, this hotel has made the transition from its former independent status to Radisson management with positive panache. A crowd of slick sophisticates drink *prosecco* and pina coladas through the afternoon from June to September, when the flashy decking often accommodates a genteel rabble of Manolo and Marc Jacobs heels during magazine bashes and sybaritic summer parties. The views over the gritty urban train tracks from neighbouring Termini inspire either love (from the

modern mavens) or hate (Grand Tour purists). Can you keep a secret? Not many know that the bar and pool are open to non-residents. Just swan up to the 7th floor in the lift, choose your sun lounger, don your designer shades and click your fingers for some nice cold drinks. Heavenly, but keep it hush.

snack...

Of late, Rome has seen a dramatic development in contemporary café culture: the traditional has met with a new breed to make a mouth-watering selection of choices for the peckish.

The traditional selection is made up of old Art Deco palace cafés, once hotbeds of polemical debate but now frequented by *grandes dames* with stiff hairdos eating *petits fours*; the rustic and supremely delicious *forni* (bakeries) serving bread, *panini*, pastries and fresh pizza; and the delicatessens – cornucopias of smells, tastes and savoury temptations.

Not forgetting, of course one of Italy's most famed exports – the gelateria. Ice cream can be found on almost every corner, especially in the Centro Storico, but discerning palates head for the traditional and the best, at Giolitti and San Crispino.

Bringing things up to date are the burgeoning contemporary tea salons, trendy book bars serving light meals, brunch and wine (where you can even book your next holiday) and most recently a growth in museum and art gallery cafés, which are culturally lively and in beautiful settings.

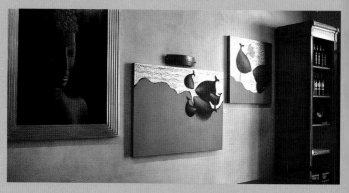

You'll find local 'bars' on every corner; it's here that most Romani will take their morning, afternoon and anytime coffee and catch up with neighbourhood gossip. Many of these bars seem cemented into a retro time warp, but they are

unrivalled portals into Roman life. One such example is the Bar San Calisto in Trastevere, which has now become a veritable institution among locals and foreigners alike and certainly warrants a visit.

Coffee etiquette is strict. The day starts with the milkiest incarnation, the cappuccino, to be taken with a *cornetto* or brioche (croissant), and after that it's pretty much *caffè* (espresso), *ristretto* (extra strong espresso) or bust. The cardinal sin is drinking a cappuccino after a meal, which, if you think about the effect of hot milk on top of a bellyful of pasta and meat, is rather logical. Put your *cognoscenti* skills into practice at Rome's best coffee house, Sant'Eustachio.

Romans are fast moving away from the sit-down two-hour lunch that leaves you supine for the rest of the afternoon, so there's a generous selection of light lunch spots and bistros for those in the know. Save the gorging for suppertime, otherwise you'll miss out on an afternoon's shopping on the Via Condotti.

Antica Enoteca della Croce, Via della Croce 76/b, Centro Storico

Tel: 06 679 0896

Open: 11.30am–1am daily.

A reliable lunchtime or *aperitivo* staple in the heart of Piazza di Spagna's

shopping paradise. The inside is spacious and cool, with wooden barrels, a high ceiling and long wooden bar boasting a vast selection of regional wines. The small menu has good salads, pastas and plates of *antipasti* treats, including cheeses and cold meats on hand round the clock.

Antico Forno Via della Scrofa, Via della Scrofa 30, Centro Storico

Open: 7am–8pm daily

Even if you are not in the least bit hungry, the fragrant odours emanating

from the *forno* on Via della Scrofa have a tendency to stop you in your tracks. This is one of the city's most ancient bakeries on one of the most ancient and atmospheric

streets. Look for the ceramic pig ('scrofa' means 'sow') whose trotter has been worn out from fortune seeking strokers. The prize draw here is the freshly baked courgette pizza, or the honeyed *cantuccini* biscuits. Sign language will come in useful, as English is limited. Just point to the type of pizza you want and gesture how big a slice you can muster. A word of advice – go large, you won't regret it.

Antico Forno Campo di Fiori, Campo dei Fiori 22, Centro Storico
Tel: 06 6880 6662
Open: 8am–1.30pm, 4–6pm. Closed Sundays.

Another of Rome's beloved old bakeries. Follow your nose to 'the Forno' in the corner of the market square to snack on their inimitable signature '*pizza rossa*' - a very thin slice of pizza base slathered with a layer of fresh tomato puree and olive oil. Equally popular is the '*piazza bianca*', which is pizza

bread with salt and olive oil, to be eaten out of its brown paper wrapping, under the statue of the ill-fated philosopher, Giordano Bruno, possibly to the accompaniment of a tanned young Lothario strumming on his guitar. Viva Roma.

Babington's English Tearoom, Piazza di Spagna 23, Centro Storico
Tel: 06 678 6027 www.babingtons.com
Open: 9am–8.30pm daily

Perched on the corner of the Spanish Steps, this traditional teahouse has

been serving up
French toast,
ploughman's
lunch and other
British comfort
foods since 1893.
This is a vision of
the tea ritual that
most Italians
think still goes on
in contemporary
England. Rather
bored-looking lobster-tinged couples and enthusiastic foreigners take inspiration from the bygone days of patrician Brits on the Grand Tour behind
flocked curtains and genteel tablecloths. Very old-fashioned and rather staid,
but if you're missing your cup of Earl Grey while abroad, this may really hit
the spot.

Le Bain, Via delle Botteghe Oscure 33, Centro Storico
Tel: 06 686 5673 www.lebain.it
Open: noon–2am. Closed Sundays.

On the rather run-down and rarely used strip between Largo Argentina and

Piazza Venezia, Le Bain was once a *de rigueur* nightspot for the fashionista
set. But the beat moves on, and these days Le Bain works best as a stylish

express lunch-stop: it's kitted out with crystal chandeliers, a marble bar and sumptuous sofas modelled on a glamorous French salon. Expect coiffed ladies who lunch, elegant local business types and a good value lunch buffet of light Mediterranean bites.

Bibli, Via dei Fienaroli 28, Trastevere
Tel: 06 588 4097 www.bibli.it
Open: 9am–midnight daily

Sundays were meant for strolling around Trastevere and the nearby flea market Porta Portese; and local independent bookshop Bibli is the perfect

detour for a hearty, healthy brunch. One of the first to hit the burgeoning trend of bookshop-cum-cafés, they offer up a fashionable spread of healthy cuisine in a cultured atmosphere. Internet access and regular talks, discussions and readings means there are plenty of arty, intelligent types to compare designer sunglasses with. A small covered garden is perfect for lazy lunches but book a table for weekend brunch, when the rafters are filled with hungry buffet bingers.

La Bottega del Caffè, Piazza Madonna dei Monti 5, Centro Storico
Open: 8am–12pm daily

This café occupies the prime position in the epicentre of the Monti neighbourhood, making it ideal for a quick, simple lunch or shopping break while you're exploring the district. At lunchtime the square comes alive with stu-

dents and bohemians eating pizza by the fountain, while later on it becomes a pleasant sun-trap during Rome's golden hour. Inside, an original stripped wooden ceiling, unfussy wooden tables and zebra-print chairs create a contemporary atmosphere, and while service is fairly slow, the cakes, desserts and atmosphere are all excellent.

Caffè Capitolino, Piazza del Campidoglio 1, Centro Storico
Tel: 06 6919 0564
Open: 9am–8pm. Closed Mondays.

As long as you don't mind sharing the view with tourists clutching oversized cameras, then this giant panoramic terrace on the kitsch Vittorio Emanuele monument in Piazza Venezia boasts one of the most consummate views of Rome. The route to the café has a pleasingly secretive air about it. From Campidoglio square, with the equestrian monument of Marcus Aurelius, take

the stairs up to the convent that are on the left, sneak through the open door on the right and follow the internal corridor along. You'll arrive in the huge terrace as if by accident. It's somewhere to quench your thirst and have a piece of cake rather than stop for lunch, but the unrivalled view and position makes it worth a look. When the sky is clear enough you can even see the Castelli Romani in the background.

Caffè delle Arti, Via A. Gramsci 73, Centro Storico
Tel: 06 3265 1236
Open: 7.45am–6pm daily

Escape from the frenetic Centro Storico and bury yourself away in the heart of the Villa Borghese. Heavenly on a hot day, this glamorous neo-classi-

cal café/restaurant adjoins the under-rated, rarely busy modern art gallery. Food may be a little average and service somewhat erratic, but the location is perfect for culture vultures swigging pitchers of wine in the midday sun under canvas awnings. A tempting array of cakes and pastries makes it a good tea-time spot when the weather is less clement, and the well-stocked bookshop next door is well worth a look.

Caffeteria d'Art al Chiostro del Bramante, Via della Pace 26, Centro Storico
Tel: 06 6880 9035 www.chiostrodelbramante.it
Open: 10am–6pm. Closed Mondays.

How do you like your eggs at the weekend? This gorgeous café sits on top of Bramante's baroque cloister next to the church of Santa Maria della Pace, and does an impressive line in scrambled eggs and omelettes among other tasty snacks. Lunches are quick and light with salads and daily specials, but

you'll want to linger, immersed in the peaceful, contemplative silence. Brunch is served at weekends until the civilized hour of 4pm. The beauty of this particular museum café is that you don't need to queue or pay to enter the gallery in order to enjoy the cloister. It's a real shame it's not open in the evenings, but tea and cakes are a close second.

Caffè Universale, Via delle Coppelle 16/a, Centro Storico
Tel: 06 6839 2065   www.universalecaffe.it
Open: 10am–11pm daily

This new café adjoins Rome's newest and biggest *hammam* (Turkish bath) in

a little street behind the Pantheon. It follows the trend of Rome's book bars, harbouring rather lofty inspirations to recreate the literary scene of the Old European cafés of

the 1930s via caffeine and conversation. Since it's attached to the Acanto day spa (see Play), its focus teeters towards the healthy and organic, but not aggressively enough to make things tedious. Rare Jamaican blends of coffee and other specialty produce including teas, wines and (oddly) pepper accompany a varied selection of books, ranging from history to contemporary literature. There's lots of relaxed Art Deco-esque seating at the back if you fancy a pleasant couple of cappuccino-soaked hours.

Ciampini, Piazza de San Lorenzo Lucina 29, Centro Storico
Tel: 06 687 6606
Open: 8am–11pm daily

This café lurks in the corner of one of the city's most sumptuous pedestrianized squares off the Via del Corso, opposite what must be Rome's most bling police station. This is civilized Rome in all its glory. Put on your new designer shades and treat your wearied feet to a *prosecco* or Campari, and enjoy the *beau-monde* merry-go-round while nibbling on an elegant selection of snacks. Everything you didn't know you could possibly want is here, from the slick magazine kiosk to Bottega Veneta next door and the pretty pharmacy (which stocks cult Kiehl's products).

Cul de Sac, Piazza Pasquino 73, Centro Storico
Tel: 06 6880 1094
Open: noon–4pm, 7–12.30am daily

An original classic. This contemporary Roman wine bar, opened in 1968, sees everyone, from footballers, design denizens and enthusiastic locals, pass through its doors. Inside the décor is simple and fairly cramped, with shared banquette seating, but the no-booking policy still makes tables hard to guarantee. The ever-evolving selection of wines is one of the best in the city and

affords plenty of experimentation. Salads, cheeses and cold meats are the speciality here, and satisfying and hearty pasta and rice dishes from northern Italy provide excellent winter comfort food. Ask for a menu in English to navigate your way through the bounteous selection of cheeses and cold cuts, and also bear in mind that the lentil soup is extraordinarily good after a night of excess.

Fabrica, Via G. Savonarola 8, Prati
Tel: 06 3972 5514 www.fabricadicalisto.com
Open: 7.30am–midnight. Closed Mondays.

The best thing to happen to Prati for quite some time is Fabrica, an ex-factory turned patisserie cum bistro cum art gallery. Navigate your way through fish entrails and fruit just off Via Andrea Doria's colourful, odiferous

outdoor market and enter the unstuffy and relaxing loft space. Run by two brothers and a sister, inside it is kitted out with monthly art shows from international artists. Exposed air vents and the central wooden bar give it a Manhattan feel, but vintage touches such as bonbons on the counter and an old set of weighing scales recall the family's patisserie past. 'High tea' is restyled and served from 9pm, whereas brunch at the weekends is a satisfying buffet served till the civilized hour of 4pm, with a live jazz accompaniment. The comforting beverages on offer range from hot chocolate with Baileys to rum and hazelnut coffees, or stop by when there's an evening vernissage and choose from margaritas, pina coladas, an ample selection of wines from every region of Italy and an eye-watering collection of grappas.

Forno La Renella, Via del Moro 15–16, Trastevere
Tel: 06 581 72 65
Open: 8am–8pm daily

It's a known hazard – if you're bar-hopping in Trastevere, dinner often gets superseded by cocktails. In this likely eventuality a munch of late-night pizza

is often a godsend, especially from the likes of this rustic bakery on Via del Moro. There are two entrances, so if you get chased in by an ardent admirer you can always escape through the back door.

Franchi, Via Cola di Rienzo, Prati
Tel: 06 686 4576
Open: 9am–8pm daily

In the heart of high bourgeois haven Prati, where the sound of Ferragamo heels combines with the patter of designer pooches' paws, you'll find this

gastronomic emporium of delights. A kaleidoscope of sweets fills the shop windows while inside is an Aladdin's cave of products for ex-pats looking for everything from Mexican relishes to Marmite. Queue up next door for take-away hot dishes

such as lasagne, stuffed tomatoes and other classic Mediterranean fodder.

Gelateria di San Crispino, Via della Panetteria 42, Centro Storico
Tel: 06 679 3924
Open: noon–12.30am. Closed Tuesdays and mid-Jan–mid-Feb.

Unfortunately there are precious few reasons for visiting the Trevi fountain these days – it's a seething pit of sweaty crowds, rose-peddlers and tacky gift shops – but its proximity to the Gelateria di San Crispino is one of them (along with a peek at papal baroque urban planning). Forget what you

think you know about ice cream and disregard the poor imitations that pepper nearly every Italian city; even in Rome there are only a handful of places worth sampling (see Ciampini and Giolitti). The Gelateria di San Crispino is notori-

ously tricky to find: proceed up Via del Tritone. till you get to the *profumeria* on the corner (with wigs in the window) and hook a left. Behind an unassuming door a cornucopia of fresh flavours and sorbets wait to change your opinion forever. It's a lesson in ice cream, and don't be alarmed by the sludgy colours (the pistachio flavour is grey rather than green). This is the watermark for determining the freshness, quality and absence of additives. Flavours change according to season, but the signature favourite is San Crispino, made from wild Sardinian honey.

Gelateria Giolitti, Via degli Uffici del Vicario 40, Centro Storico

Tel: 06 699 1243
Open: 7am–2am daily

Despite the hordes that populate Rome's most famous gelateria, it's certainly worth queuing behind the sweaty crowds for this unadulterated ice-cream experience. Giolitti has been in business since 1900 and the style of

this classic ice-cream parlour has changed very little since the turn of the century – it looks splendid. Beat the crowds, cool off in the cool *belle époque* marble interior and treat yourself to a sundae or perhaps the famous Sicilian *cassata* ice-cream cake. It may be a little more pricey but you're sure to be served with more haste and get a chance to soak up the retro glamour under the chandeliers.

Gina, Via S.Sebastianello 7/A, Villa Borghese

Tel: 06 678 0251   www.ginaroma.com
Open: 11am–midnight (8pm Sun) daily

This sleek, fashionable eaterie behind the claustrophobic Spanish Steps positively screams Chelsea and is frequented by a similar brigade of Pilates-honed and expensively highlighted types, who nibble away at salads. For

those with a more hearty constitution a good selection of comforting soups and satisfying *panini* really hits the spot. When summer beckons, picnic hampers with sandwiches and fruit salad are on hand for customers to take up to the Villa Borghese gardens. Practise your air-kissing, pull up a pew next to the nearest blonde *Big Brother* starlet and watch the traffic of beautiful people ebb and flow.

L'Impiccione Viaggiatore, Via Madonna dei Monti 28, Monti

Tel: 06 678 6188   www.limpiccioneviaggiatore.com
Open: 10am–midnight. Closed Mondays.

An innovative venue based in up-and-coming Monti, this schizophrenic store incorporates a travel agency, bookshop, art gallery restaurant and café all in one delightful bundle. Owner Danilo will single-handedly organize your holiday for two in the Maldives while you browse brochures and let your taste buds travel across continents with an international selection of wine. But even if your pocket doesn't permit spa-hopping in Uruguay this travel concept store specifically caters for the armchair traveller who is loath to leave the Bel Paese. Wanderlust is sated through monthly themed seasons around specific countries, with talks from local architects, photo exhibitions

and food tasting. Wireless internet throughout allows further dreaming of far-flung destinations with a comprehensive selection of travel literature to pore over while you enjoy a coffee and one of the fresh home-made pastries and cakes.

Mimi e Cocco, Via del Governo Vecchio 72, Centro Storico
Tel: 06 6821 0845
Open: 10am–10pm daily

A friendly neighbourhood vibe permeates this cosy café, making it a welcome spot to stop for snack while vintage shopping on Via del Governo

Vecchio. Inside it's intimate: you'll normally find a smattering of cool old dudes, trendy locals and the occasional glamour-puss spilling out onto the street. Fresh salads, soups, crêpes, pasta and rice dishes are served with an

easy-going attitude that inspires lingering. Enjoy the extensive tea and wine list and take time to chat to convivial owner Andrea, who revels in the chance to practise his English on unsuspecting diners.

Obika' Piazza di Firenze, Via dei Prefetti, Centro Storico
Tel: 06 683 2630 www.obika.it
Open: 8am–midnight daily

As those connoisseurs of the white, milky cheese will readily tell you, there's more to mozzarella than topping a pizza or sliced in a *caprese* salad. Considered to be the first mozzarella bar in the world, Obika' serves soft,

succulent *mozzarella di bufala* fresh every day from Campania in a variety of incarnations. Gorge yourself on a classic ball of *bufala*, accompanied by anything from ham, tomatoes and pesto to *bottarga*, capers and anchovies. Other Italian specialities from DOP regions include wild boar salami, *mortadella* and an extensive wine list. The salads are gargantuan and daily pasta, soup and rice specials offer alternatives to cheese. Sit in the pretty piazza outside or the mercifully air-conditioned interior – a fusion of Japanese styling with some ancient-looking columns supporting the minimalist structure. Obika' attracts a business lunch crowd, a smart *aperitivo* set and general aficionados of the white stuff. Just so you feel like one of the *cognoscenti* in cheese circles, *mozzarella di bufala* is from the milk of the water buffalo, while *fior di latte* mozzarella is made from humble cow's milk.

Palazzetto International Wine Academy, Vicolo del Bottino 8, Centro Storico

Tel: 06 699 0878

Open: noon–11pm daily

This sophisticated little spot is possibly one of the best-kept secrets in Rome. Ancillary to the über-posh Hotel Hassler and owned by the same Robert Wirth, the Palazzetto sits on the side of the famous Spanish Steps in

the throbbing heart of the Centro Storico. This place positively reeks of moneyed refinement, but surprisingly lacks the prohibitive prices that one might have expect- ed. Lunch is served on the terrace

between noon and 4pm, the only public space to overlook the Spanish Steps. The cosy bar is open till well after dinner, and resembles a gentle- men's study with backgammon and vintage chessboards. You're most likely to encounter the residents of the four rooms that make up the Palazzetto's boutique hotel and other smug, in-the-know sybarites.

Pupina, Via Marianna Dionigi 37, Prati

Tel: 06 322 3338   www.pupina.it

Open: 8am–11.30pm. Closed on Sundays and throughout August.

This bistro, with its white wicker chairs, lovely lighting and touches of blue and red, has a fresh and bright, almost French feeling. Lunch is a consistently delicious affair with abundant salads and dishes of the day, with plenty of creative vegetarian choices. Emphasis is on healthy, light yet extremely tasty cuisine and there's always a fabulous selection of daily dessert specials. Popular with the Prati gang and workers from around Piazza Cavour, it makes a pleasant interlude between Vatican sightseeing and shopping on Via Cola di Rienzo and is perfect for an express lunch. Presiding over it at

lunchtimes is a super-efficient and supercilious manager, who never fails to accommodate with his own Basil Fawlty-esque hotelier breed of charm.

Rivendita, Vicolo del Cinque 11/a, Trastevere
Tel: 06 5830 1868 www.cioccolataevino.com
Open: 10am–2am. Closed Mondays.

Chocolates, coffee, wine and books all have their individual merits but when all four combine in one of the coolest boho spots in the city it makes for sheer indulgence. This tiny bar positively sizzles with a cool crowd with a sweet tooth, who stop off after dinner for a caffeine fix and that seductive last glass of wine. Feed your imagination with a selection of battered books, all under €5, and watch the sexy, dishevelled crowds teeter by. Skip dessert and coffee elsewhere and take it here, if you can, snatching one of the

battered armchairs flung onto the cobbles outside. One glance at the staff and clientele and you might get the feeling that this place opened in response to the late-night munchies.

Rosati, Piazza del Popolo 5, Centro Storico
Tel: 06 322 5859
Open: 8am–11.30pm daily

Once the haunt of intellectuals from Pasolini to Italo Calvino, this art nouveau café no longer fizzes with left-wing polemics, but its ringside views of Piazza del Popolo, old-fashioned cocktails and teatime treats still make it

a very civilized spot. Pop in at breakfast-time for a brioche and cappuccino or before dinner for an old-school cocktail. The *Sogni Romani* is the signature drink made with orange juice and red and yellow liqueurs, to mimic the colours of the city and the Roma football team.

Sant'Eustachio, Piazza Sant'Eustachio 82, Centro Storico
Tel: 06 686 1309
Open: 8am–8pm daily

In a country lubricated by daily doses of caffeine, competition for supremacy is fierce, but many would vociferously argue that Sant'Eustachio boasts the best coffee in Rome. The 100% Arabica beans are roasted over wood on site and make their way into the retro 1940s interior to be served up in all their gloriously smooth incarnations from espresso to cappuccino by the skilled and solemn *baristi*. The classic tipple here is the *gran caffè lungo*, which comes with a layer of burnished creamy foam on its slick mahogany base. This is not a place to linger – coffee etiquette demands a maximum of 5

minutes at the bar – but if you do pull up a pew on the outside tables be warned that there is, as ever, a steep mark up in prices for the pleasure.

Sciam, Via del Pellegrino 56, Centro Storico
Tel: 06 6830 8957
Open: 4pm–2am daily

When you're bored of baroque architecture and tales of antiquity it may be time to rock the kazbar on the other side of Campo dei Fiori. Thankfully this Middle Eastern café lacks any screaming old rocker types, perhaps

because they don't serve alcohol. Kick back on some cushions out of the afternoon sun, have a chat over an aromatic fruit tobacco water pipe ('*narghile*'), snack on some *baba ganoush* and lentils, and drink herbal infusions and mango juice till late. Kitsch touches and a relaxing vibe with colourful characters, especially from the Ottoman carpet shop next door.

Tad Café, Via del Babuino 155/a, Centro Storico
Tel: 06 3269 5123
Open: 10am–7.30pm daily

Rome's lifestyle concept-store Tad is a retail compendium of fabulous shoes, designer garments, small label luxury cosmetics and perfumes, magazines, books, CDs and exotic home furnishings. If that weren't enough you can

extend your experience in Tad-world by stopping off for a tasty bite in the café at the back, perhaps consoling yourself with some of their scrumptious cakes (from a choice of 50) if that Balenciaga dress doesn't quite fit.

Thè Verde, Via Bocca di Leone 46, Centro Storico
Tel: 06 6992 3705
Open: 10am–9pm. Closed Sundays.

An oriental-inspired teahouse that offers a clement and refreshing respite from pounding the shopping streets around Via dei Condotti. It's contemporary rather than traditional, and you can choose from over 100 types of teas and infusions, chocolates and coffees; if you still need to satisfy those revived retail urges after that, there's a boutique of teapots, garments and oriental knick-knacks to keep you satisfied. Light yet satisfying lunches and enticing desserts are also served in the open-air restaurant and on a handful of tables scattered on the cobbles outside. Tranquil throughout the day but

buzzy early evening, when it becomes a lovely spot for a glass of wine after all that credit-card flexing.

Volpetti Tavola Calda and Deli, Via Marmorata 47, Trastevere

Tel: 06 574 2352 www.volpetti.com
Open: 8am–2pm, 4–8pm. Closed Tuesday afternoons and Sundays.

Boisterous, bustling and fun, this is the ultimate Italian delicatessen experience in a rather more rustic part of town, so sign language may come in handy here. Salivate over hung hams and pungent cheeses and collect a smorgasbord of treats before scaling the nearby Aventine for a picnic in the Orange gardens. The fresh slabs of

pizza cooked on site have dense, juicy toppings, but you could try the speciality here, 'corallina' – a lean pork and lard spicy salami, popular at Easter. If the weather doesn't permit al fresco snacking, go round the corner to Volpetti Tavola Calda for all the signature ingredients served in a rough-and-ready cafeteria.

Notes & Updates

party...

Those coming to Rome to go wild in fabulously fashionable nightclubs may be disappointed, since on the whole the club scene remains commercial or still entrenched in that breed of euro house music that was successful in the drugged-up 1990s. Romans can be rather provincial in their tastes, so while music is mostly contemporary, only a handful of venues feel cutting-edge.

It's quality rather than quantity here, and venues range from chic and sophisticated, to unapologetically cheesy, to interestingly leftfield – or more often than not, a schizophrenic mix of all three.

Thursdays to Sundays are the big nights out and, as in most of Europe, don't even dream of stepping out before midnight. The routine is vigorously thus: *aperitivo*, followed by dinner with lashings of wine, then a coffee and pick-me-up in a bar before it's time (remember – not before midnight) to jostle your way into your venue of choice.

The hub of Rome's nightlife is concentrated around the Monte di Testaccio hill and old slaughterhouse, where a never-ending strip of bars and clubs leads from the Via Galvani around the hill. If you want to keep life simple, head here – you'll be spoilt for choice. For a grittier, splinter scene, explore the Via Libetta around the corner in the up-and-coming neighbourhood of Ostiense.

Centro Storico keeps things chic and glamorous with baroque décor and chandeliers at La Maison, Bloom and La Cabala. Alternatively you can relive traditional *dolce vita* decadence at old-time favourites Jackie O and Gilda.

As an antidote to the sleek and coiffed brand of clubbing, the Centro Sociali offer an alternative scene. These formerly abandoned buildings have been occupied by collectives with a political and social activist agenda. Some can be a little hard-edged, but they often have the most discerning music and provide an interesting snapshot into organized cultural chaos in the Eternal City. The best are Brancaleone and Rialto San Ambrogio.

There is an often confusing 'consummazione' system in operation in most clubs, where the price of entry (anywhere between €5 and €25) often includes the price of your first drink. You may also be presented with a 'tessera' or drinks card, which will be stamped at the bar with every drink. You then present your card at the 'cassa' when you leave to pay for what you've consumed, to often disconcerting effect. A word of warning: if you lose the tessera during the course of the evening you'll be subject to paying the full quota.

From June onwards most of the city's clubs close down completely or migrate to the nearby beaches of Ostia and Fregene, and a trip out to the coast may prove a little impractical unless you have a car and are teetotal. But all is not lost. Summer in the city is all about cocktail-quaffing on hotel rooftops or lingering till late in piazzas and wine bars in the balmy Roman night. You may find you don't want to tear yourself away.

Finally, keep your eyes and nose keen on the way home and indulge in a cappuccino and fresh brioche at 4am, when the bakeries start to churn out the first batch of the day. They beat a kebab hands down.

Weekly details can be found in the listings magazine Roma C'è available on newsstands.

Akab, Via Monte Testaccio 69, Testaccio

Tel: 06 578 2390

Open: 11pm–4.30am. Closed Mondays.

Akab is a sort of everyman nightspot which manages to tick most boxes for an entertaining night out. Caved into the Monte dei Cocci in Testaccio it seems endless in its sprawl. Drink and shimmy in the covered garden then descend into the cavernous rooms below for a more clubby atmosphere, and if you get bored, check out the third room upstairs. The best nights for the real Romani are on a Tuesday with the L-Ektrica electro party and

Convista on a Sunday night. Fridays and Saturdays are busy and more commercial without being too cheesy.

Art Café, Viale del Galoppatoio 33, Villa Borghese

Tel: 06 3600 6578

Open: 9pm–3am daily. Closed July–September.

This club has a rather unusual location, situated under the Villa Borghese car park, and seeming as if it's in a shopping centre, but the Romans appear to be oblivious to the fact that this could be incongruous with the stylish shenanigans they promote inside. Art Café draws a youngish crowd of male and female label-sluts, which isn't surprising seeing as the club hosts various self-conscious fashion events. During the warmer months the dance-floor moves out under the trees and stars of Villa Borghese where it is served by a cocktail bar in the garden. You can also dine in decadence at the Art Café – to a jazz accompaniment on a Thursday while Friday is a bombastically bling hip-hop night (Roma style). If you're used to clubbing in London and New York you may find it just a little naïve, but it does draw a trendy crowd of flamboyant young pretty things who just want to have fun.

Expect future Miss Italias, boys in distressed jeans and loud shirts and a healthy dose of Roberto Cavalli.

Brancaleone, Via Levanna 11, Villa Borghese
Tel: 06 8200 4382 www.brancaleone.it
Open: times vary Weds–Sat. Closed August.

Perhaps the leading *centro sociale* in Rome, 'Branca' has been providing alternative musical entertainment and social happenings since 1990. Once an abandoned *palazzo* with non-profit social activist intentions, the space has seen a restyling with modern lighting and bar area. The initial anti-establishment philosophy has remained, with a prolific agenda of theatre, dance,

video-art and multi-media events combined with banging club nights hosting US, European and Japanese acts and DJs. The crowd are cool, very cool, but if you're not well versed on Bolivian socio-economic politics, avoid striking up a conversation with the bearded revellers – you may feel out of your depth. This is a place for specialists, musically and culturally. Firewater Wednesday nights see DJs from Layo and Bushwacka to Groove Armada grace the decks. For dance music aficionados, Friday hosts the legendary Agatha party, Saturday is Microhouse, and Thursday the One Love Hi Pawa party with dance hall and reggae. It's urban and unostentatious, with not a whiff of Cavalli in sight, but the drawback is that since it's all the way out on the Via Salaria you will need a taxi.

La Cabala, Via dei Soldati 24/c, Centro Storico
Tel: 06 6830 1192
Open: 11pm–3am. Closed Mondays, July and August

This former 1970s boogie nights beat-box has reopened to centro storico revellers with rather startling success. Nestled above the Hostaria dell'Orso restaurant in a 15th-century palazzo, the dance club boasts a uniquely atmospheric location with views glimpsing the Tevere through stain-glassed

windows. Whatever religious mysticism the name may suggest don't go looking for Madonna and other spiritually affected divas, if anything La Cabala is a ministry of former (rather than future) Miss Italias. Ignore the somewhat poncey piano bar on the ground floor, come suited and booted, preferably with Gina Lollobrigida, and get ready to burn off the pasta pounds.

Classico Village, Via Libetta 3, Rome

Tel: 06 574 3364 www.classicovillage.net
Open: 9pm–3am. Closed Mondays.

This former factory is one of Ostiense's most popular nightspots, which, with its restaurant, stage for live bands, club area and courtyard bar (that becomes particularly delectable in the summer), really does resemble a nocturnal village. Denizens of the DJ circuit ranging from Felix da Housecat to Jazzanova play marathon sets to an uplifted, un-coiffed crowd. An adjoining restaurant cooks up simple classic clubbers' delights to provide the calories

for all that bouncing. Take your pick from the vigorous Moka Black Express on a Friday night and varied special sets on a Saturday. Jazz nights and rock gigs also make up the musical programme.

Goa, Via Libetta 13, Rome

Tel: 06 574 8277
Open: 11pm–4am. Closed Sundays and Mondays, July and August.

Lost nights in some trance-music bubble on the beaches of the Asian subcontinent? The name of this club says it all. Less crusty, no sand but still as ravey, this is the superstar DJ venue *par choix* in Rome, with king of Italo-House Claudio Coccoluto at its throne. Expect pernickety VIP areas, ethno-Bollywood-inspired interiors and an awesome sound system – you go to dance rather than chat, as the sound is deafening. It's strictly for devotees of the repetitive beat, since the music can be quite hard, but an international programme of DJs keeps a sexy young 20- to 30-something crowd arriving

in hordes. Thursday nights go electro, while Saturday sees the house-heads come out for an ear-splitting rave.

Gilda, Via Mario de' Fiori 97, Centro Storico
Tel: 06 678 4838
Open: 9.30pm–4am. Closed July–September.

Gloriously out of date, this is one of Rome's historic nightclubs, with all the trimmings. Named after Rita Hayworth's best-known cinematic role, it's all red velvet curtains, self-important bouncers in black-tie and flashy styling. Verging on the camp, the parties range from Serie A footballers' nights to themed signs of the zodiac evenings. The Ristorante Le Cru and sushi bar attracts a well-heeled, slightly more mature Euro jet-set who content themselves by mingling with past politicians and minor VIPs. Good, clean, cheesy yet expensive fun.

Don't even dream of turning up in jeans and cool imported trainers – jackets and shoes are required. So if you can't modernize them, join them. Order buckets of champagne and enjoy.

Jackie-O, Via dei Boncompagni, Via Veneto
Tel: 06 4288 5457
Open: 10pm–late Tues–Sat

Once upon a time the covered walkway at Jackie O's entrance saw a catwalk of international celluloid stars from the 1960s and '70s shimmy through the gates and into this celebrated piano bar/club. Today's crowd are mostly those clinging on by their decaying talons to that bygone era of decadent Roman nightlife, but remarkably it's still quite a laugh. The music is an entertaining selection of 1970s commercial to contemporary chart. It's so cheesy that

some promoters have taken to it with postmodern ironic glee, taking the opportunity to organize one-off parties for trendier types. But on every other night it's a staunch brigade of polo necks and blazers, fur coats and hairspray, and discreet, if sneering barmen. Brilliant for not changing one little bit.

Joia, Via Galvani 20, Testaccio
Tel: 06 574 0802   www.joiacafe.it
Open: 8pm–late. Closed Mondays.

One of the better venues around Testaccio's nightlife strip, Joia is right in the thick of Via Galvani, close to the Piramide. A consistently rammed dance-floor and big queues to get in to get on are set off by a pleasant outdoor area with rooftop dining, although the service can be average to appalling. There are rather a lot of eager men, some very dressed-up girls and lots of posing on the cramped, swarming terrace. Music is fun and you're pretty much guaranteed a good dance to contemporary commercial tunes. You'll find a piano bar and cream-furnished salon on the first floor – but if you want to snack and sup on champagne here (not a bad option), you have to

book. Up another level (getting up the stairs when it's busy is like struggling against salmon swimming upstream) is the summer dance-floor and outside terrace. Black-and-white images of screen sirens decorate the cream walls in the summer terrace while imperial Russian reds decorate the disco downstairs. Be prepared to spend on drinks.

La Maison, Vicolo dei Granari 4, Centro Storico
Tel: 06 683 3312
Open: 11pm–5am. Closed Mondays and June–September.

Probably the best nightclub to be found in Centro Storico – if you *can* find it, that is. La Maison lurks down a tiny, atmospheric *vicolo* in between Piazza

Navona and Via del Governo Vecchio. But once you get close you'll know you've arrived as there's always a scrum at the door. This makes for a fairly contrary door policy, so dress up, act confidently and look like you're going to spend some money. That said, if you're a woman under 35, you won't have any problems at all. Once inside the door, get ready to play – two neo-baroque rooms are at your pleasure, bedecked in velvet and dripping with chandeliers. Gilded mirrors afford practised posing to accommodate those Italian egos, and let you see when you've had one too many and your head's about to fall off (drinks are very strong). When the best party is on a Sunday night, you know the kind of decadent crowd to expect, and Flavia Lazzarini's Glamnight is the most *à la mode*, lightly transgressive house party in town. Go shake your tail feather.

Micca Club, Via Pietro Micca 7/a, Monti

Tel: 06 8744 0079 www.miccaclub.com
Open: 10pm–3am Wed–Sat. Closed August.

Micca Club is testament to the cultural expansion of the former no man's land flanking Termini around Piazza Vittorio. This club complex is the baby of the Gruppo Innocenti Hotels and proposes an innovative take on club-bing. With burlesque and themed 1920s nights it feels like Micca has taken

its lead from vanguard Berlin, London or New York clubs. Of course you can't erase that charming mix of Euro sleaze/cheese entirely (but then again, who would want to?). Not content with a crowd pleasing club nights and a varied live music programme, they also boast their own online radio station and maga-zine, produced within the 600sq m flagship. In fact it's a whole Micca world, with a Sunday afternoon vintage vinyl and clothes market.

Modo, Vivolo del Fico 3, Centro Storico
Tel: 06 686 7452 www.modo.roma.it
Open: 6pm–2am daily. Closed July and August.

This little venue off Piazza del Fico is very conveniently located for a spot of live music and partying every night of the week, with DJs at weekends. Small but perfectly formed, this newcomer to the Roman club scene takes its

music seriously. Blacked-out interiors and a chrome bar distinguish it from the more usual chandeliered temples to the boogie that you'll find locally. Its novelty has made it popular with the trendy night owls who haunt this side of Piazza Navona, making every night a party. How long will the beat go on? Who can tell.

L'Oppio, Via delle Terme di Tito 72, Monti
Tel: 06 474 5262 www.oppiocaffe.it
Open: 7pm–3am daily

On a terrace overlooking the Forum and Colosseum, Oppio caffè offers revellers a rare opportunity to enjoy the panorama of Ancient Rome while refuelling on booze. L'Oppio started life as a pizzeria but the adjoining late-night bar has become a distinguished hotspot for bright young things from *aperitivo* hour onwards. It takes its name from the hill on which it sits, the Esquiline, or Mons Oppius. And the musical offerings are varied, from the 'Je Suis Sublime' night featuring French music from the 1970s through to Mc Solaar to the 'House of Love' parties, 'African Beats' and 'Groove Anthology' nights with the best of nu-wave house music. A friendly, unpretentious con-

temporary crowd dance to the beat as the sun goes down on *caput mundi*.

Orpheus, Via Monte di Testaccio 53, Testaccio

Tel: 06 5730 1637

Open: Closed Mondays.

The clubs along the strip of Monte di Testaccio have fairly little to distinguish them from one another, but the terrace at Orpheus, with its incandescent neon light projections, is sheer, uncomplicated fun. With its PVC-clad dancer shaking her thing on a podium, it may lean towards the tacky, but somehow it really doesn't matter. Cheesy boys in pink satin jackets and

wannabe tough B boys throw shapes on the decking but no one really takes themselves too seriously. The music makes the friendly crowd move with some old-school commercial classics and a rather young, easily pleased crowd. Guilty pleasures all round, really.

Rialto SanAmbrogio, Via di Sant' Ambrogio, Centro Storico

Tel: 06 6813 3640 www.rialtosantambrogio.org
Open: times vary, check the website. Closed Sundays and August.

This is probably the most exciting it gets in terms of Rome contemporary clubbing. Wedged in the backstreets of the area known as the Jewish ghetto, 'Rialto' is an example of a gritty 'centro sociali' which has evolved into the

spot for the capital's movers and shakers. Formerly a 16th-century convent, this occupied building is now religiously frequented by disciples of cool. Much more than just a nightclub, the two-storey palazzo is a whole cultural complex along the lines of what the ICA does in London with a never-ending sequence of theatre, club nights, video projections, film screenings and book launches and draws in a similar zeitgeist crowd of 20– and 30–something culture mavens. Flying the flag for the growing Italian electro scene is Condominio on the last Friday of the month with Rome's best DJ Flavia Lazzarini. But shhhh… as with all good things, try and keep it a little bit secret.

Supperclub, Via dei Nari 14, Centro Storico

Tel: 06 6830 1011 www.supperclub.com
Open: 8.30pm–2am. Closed Mondays and Tuesdays.

Love it or hate it, this slightly poncey outpost of the Amsterdam nightspot still retains a certain dominance on the Centro Storico club circuit. It's fairly pretentious and so full of rules and regulations it's almost like being on an aeroplane, with an exclusive door policy reminiscent of airport security to match. Dinner is served on white couches where guests gorge Nero-style (on rather mediocre food), while avant-garde performances take place. Rule

number one: diners must remove their shoes while eating, so leave the comedy socks at home and make sure you've had a pedicure to maintain the '*bella figura*'. The cocktail bar is festooned with heavy red drapes where stylish *baristi* serve a healthy array of cocktails, and downstairs soft neon and blindingly white walls and seating create a *Barbarella*-esque environment for dancing.

MUSIC CLUBS

Alexanderplatz, Via Ostia 9, Prati
Tel: 06 3975 1877   www.alexanderplatz.it
Open: 8pm–3am. Closed Sundays, and July–August.

Curiously named after a cattle market in Berlin (which was later used for military parades), this jazz club near the Vatican in residential, grown-up Prati has been going for over 20 years. It looks the part, in true New Orleans style, and the atmosphere is anything but pompous and formal. International jazz artists have left their mark with signatures and graffiti on the walls. Dinner is served from 9pm, with live music starting at 10.30pm. It's a different night out, but very authentic. Be sure to book.

Big Mama Jazz Club, Vicolo San Francesco a Ripa 18, Travastere

Tel: 06 581 2551 www.bigmama.it

Open: 9pm–1.30am. Closed Mondays, and July to the end of September.

Known as 'home of the blues' in Rome, this jazz club is squeezed in between tiny winding streets and churches, so maybe that's why the atmosphere is so concentrated with a discerning crowd of jazz and blues enthusiasts. There's a euphoric, underground atmosphere when jam sessions kick off, but as a result of the no smoking legislation in Italy, that romantic bluesy fog is now missing. Cocktails and dining are also an option, but food is average at best. Book a table in advance and look out for big names passing through town. Civilized and charming, and perfectly situated for a *passegiata* and nightcap in Trastevere post-gig.

La Palma, Via G. Mirri 35, Rome

Tel: 06 4359 9029 www.lapalmaclub.it

A little bit out of town, La Palma occupies an old industrial hangar and is an electric venue for bands, from jazz to rock and indie. This vast space attracts a decidedly cool crowd from town who enjoy the music, cinema screenings, international DJ sets and photo exhibitions. A cultural smorgasbord, if you will.

ADULT ENTERTAINMENT

Prostitution is illegal in Italy but the culture is so ingrained with a deep-rooted appreciation for T&A that there's no shortage of strip clubs to titillate what Italians see as those natural primal instincts. Those seeking transgressive thrills have to head either around Termini station or a little out of town to the suburbs for some *in flagrante delictorum*.

Armony Club, Via S. Vito 12, Termini

Tel: 06 446 5796 www.armonyclub.com

Discotheque, sex zone, erotic show and dark room near Termini station.

Boite Pigalle, Via dell'Umiltà 77, Rome

Tel: 06 678 5475   http://web.tiscali.it/boitepigalle/

Open: 10pm–5am. Closed Mondays.

Just off Via del Corso, a very old fashioned strip club with dancing girls, on-stage shows and the usual over-priced cocktails.

Cica Cica Boom, Via Liguria 38, Via Veneto

Tel: 06 488 4745

A classic strip club, just off Via Veneto.

Il Club di Cicciolina Via Del Tritone 132, Centro Storico

Named after the famous porn-star turned politician and cultural icon La Cicciolina.

La Villa di Grotta Ferrata, Via Montiglioni 2, Grotta Ferrata

www.lavilladigrottaferrata.it

A lavish villa and couples sex club pleasure palace just outside Rome.

Hg2 Rome

culture...

It's no exaggeration to say that Rome is one of the most culturally intense cities in the world. It would be insane to try and force yourself to see everything in one short trip when it took 2,800 years to create the palimpsest of art and architecture that you see today – you just couldn't do it. From the atmospheric ruins of Republic and Empire to the glories of papal patronage, and the neo-classical and fascist edifices of more recent times, the Rome skyline is an exciting hotch-potch of styles and timelines. Much more than a coin thrown into the Trevi fountain, this is Rome's way of making sure you keep coming back to see what you missed last time.

Art galleries in Rome are unavoidably exhausting, so prepare accordingly with bottled water, comfy shoes and patience to deal with the often clueless, ovine crowds. The Galleria Borghese, the Vatican museums and the Capitoline museums are the most gruelling because they attract the highest volume of visitors. Skipping over ruins in the aggressive sun can also be very debilitating.

As an antidote to museum agony you can make a spiritual or cultural pilgrimage to Rome's churches. Since it's the HQ of Christianity it's no surprise that Rome has more churches per capita than there are pubs in Yorkshire. They offer an infinitely more civilized way of taking in relatively crowd-free nuggets of culture, and their cool stone interiors are a soothing shelter from the searing summer heat.

The exception to this rule is of course Rome's most famous church – St Peter's Basilica, with its soaring High Renaissance dome designed by Michelangelo. Its significance ensures a year-round queue and strict security. Don't forget to dress accordingly: covered knees and shoulders for women and no shorts for men.

If the Renaissance (broadly speaking) belongs to Florence, then Rome lays claim to the exuberant, theatrical baroque style of architecture, which emerged in response to the austere Protestant Reformation. The protagonists of the style who decorated Rome were papal pet favourites Gian Lorenzo Bernini, Francesco Borromini and Pietro da Cortona.

Of late Rome has been shedding its entrenched historical heritage and waking up to the present day.
The first contemporary art museum (MACRO) opened in 1999 while construction is under way for the new MAXXI (Museum of 21st Century Art) designed by Anglo-Iraqi architect Zaha Hadid.

Just a little further out is the new auditorium, which opened in 2002 to host classical and contemporary concerts. Architect Renzo Piano (famous for the Pompidou Centre in Paris) built the Parco della Musica, with its three turtle-shaped halls boasting near-perfect acoustics and an outdoor amphitheatre.

For those nostalgic for halcyon days, head out to the leafy Appia Antica, a quiet, 4th-century BC Roman road lined with glamorous Renaissance villas and the catacombs of the long-departed. The Appia Antica starts at Porta San Sebastiano (rent a bike from the Centro Visite Parco Appia Antica, half a kilometre outside the gate), but you can take the Archeobus from Termini station, which stops at the major sights along the strip.

Think of the following as a confection of pickings to take you off in different directions rather than a comprehensive guide to Rome's cultural platter.

L'Ara Pacis, Via Ripetta, Centro Storico
Tel: 06 6880 6848
Open: 9am–7pm Tues–Sun. Closed Mondays.

The ara pacis or 'altar of peace' was inaugurated in 9 BC to celebrate the wealth and security that the emperor Augustus had brought by pacifying Gaul and Spain. The carvings of cattle, swans, insects, flowers and fruit all portray a message of peace and prosperity. The altar originally sat in the Campo Marzio somewhere around the piazza of San Lorenzo in Lucina but was destroyed when Rome fell to the Barbarians. Mussolini ordered the

reconstruction of the altar in the late 1930s, assembling the fragments from excavations and pieces scattered in European museums, and housed it on the banks of the Tiber. The newly restored structure designed to display the ara pacis was by Richard Meyer. The protective structure made from travertine marble, large glass panes and metal bars has received a mixed, and at times vociferous, reception.

Capitoline Museums, Piazza del Campidoglio 1, Via Veneto and Villa Borghese
Tel: 06 6710 2071 www.museicapitolini.org
Open: 9am–8pm (last entry 7pm). Closed Mondays.

This is one of the oldest public museums in the world, starting life in 1471 when benevolent Pope Sixtus IV decided to bestow upon the city a collection of bronze sculptures. The museum finally opened to the public in 1734. The bronze equestrian statue of Marcus Aurelius set dramatically in the square is a copy of the 2nd-century AD original inside. Entrance to the collection is through the Palazzo dei Conservatori on the right of Michelangelo's piazza and staircase. Highlights include the Spinario in Room

3, a 1st-century BC bronze of a young boy removing a thorn from his foot, which is probably a Greek work. Room 4 has the much-reproduced Roman she-wolf, who suckled the twins Romulus and Remus, while Bernini's snake-infested Medusa head is in Room 5. The picture gallery has a few significant pieces, particularly Caravaggio's painting of John the Baptist grappling with a ram. If it weren't for the title it would be hard to see how this painting is holy – the figure is stripped of any religious context. The Palazzo Nuovo on the other side of the square houses ancient sculpture, with portrait busts of Roman citizens displaying their changing hairstyles and fashions. There's the 1st-century BC Capitoline Venus, most likely based on an ancient sculpture called the Venus of Cnodis, who was considered so erotic that one Greek citizen was found having a smooch with the marble babe.

Centrale Montemartini, Via Ostiense 106, Ostiense
Tel: 06 3996 7800 www.centralemontemartini.org
Open: 9am–7pm. Closed Mondays.

This museum is a fascinating antidote to the well-trodden culture trail and is a good excuse to get out to Ostiense, an up-and-coming (and fashionably gritty) area of Rome. The museum started life as an electricity plant in 1912, but some bright spark had the idea of housing the overspill of classical sculpture from the Capitoline museums into the later defunct space. The result is remarkable: Roman busts perch on turbines and marble muses sit

comfortably next to diesel engines. It fits in perfectly with the local urban chic elite and is sure to swell with visitors once Rem Koolhaus starts his project for regenerating the disused Mercati Generali over the road. For the moment, however, it feels like a fabulously well-kept secret. The café on the third floor also serves a mean brunch.

Colosseum, Piazza del Colosseo, Via Veneto
Tel: 06 700 5469
Open: 9am–sunset daily

Work got under way for the Colosseum in AD 72 and took a mere eight years to complete, thanks mostly to slave labour. Its name refers to its 'colossal' size but also to a giant gold plated statute imitating the Colossus at Rhodes, which once stood next to the stadium. The building is 500 meters in diameter and was inaugurated in AD 80, with a blockbuster '100

Days of Carnage' to whet the appetite of the populus romanus. Gory battles between gladiators, slaves, wild animals and prisoners in different combinations comprised the entertainment programme, but towards the decline of the Roman Empire the action was reduced to less heroic battles between chickens pecking each other to shreds. The Colosseum could seat 50,000 spectators and entrance was free to all. This made it an integral part of the 'bread and circuses' strategy to keep citizens pacified, the reasoning being that if a populace have enough to eat and are entertained, then they're less likely to revolt.

Fori Imperiali, Via dei Fori Imperiali, Centro Storico
Open: 9.30–6pm daily. Guided tours in English 3pm Wed, Sat, Sun.

The area known as the Forum was the nucleus of urban Roman life where everything, from commerce and business to prostitution and the administration of justice, took place, and where news and announcements were disseminated. The site started off as soggy marshland between the Capitoline

and Palatine hills, but was drained and then paved with travertine marble during the reign of Augustus. The Fori are a complex patchwork of ruins of significant buildings that include temples, basilicas and triumphal arches, as well as the Curia, which was home to the Senate. The Temple of Saturn is one of the oldest, dating from 500 BC, and also acted as the treasury storing the Empire's gold and silver. Another vast structure is the former Basilica of Maxentius and Constantine, a court house, council chamber and meeting-place. When Christianity was legalized in AD 313 the first Christian meeting-places were often former basilicas, which is why the term 'basilica' is

165

often associated with churches. The street running to the Colosseum is known as the Via Sacra and was often used for processions. Unfortunately Mussolini carved through centuries' worth of architectural debris in the 1930s to build the Via dei Fori Imperiali thoroughfare, which slices the site of the Forum in two. This was originally known as 'Empire Street' to fulfil the dictator's own imperialistic pretensions.

Galleria d'Arte Moderna, Viale delle Belle Arti 131, Villa Borghese

Tel: 06 322 981   www.gnam.arti.beniculturali.it/gnamco.htm
Open: 8.30am–7.30pm. Closed Mondays.

This palatial neo-classical building is often neglected in favour of the Museo Borghese on the other side of the park, but it makes a dramatic antidote to Renaissance and baroque architecture, not to mention the glorious ruins of Ancient Rome. Seventy-five relatively crowd-free rooms house Italy's largest collection of home-grown 19th- and 20th-century art that includes Boccioni, Morandi, Fontana and Modigliani. Other nations enjoy considerable representation with works by Klimt, Kandinsky, Pollock, Mondrian and Van

Gogh, while the sculpture collection is particularly strong with some Rodin and Henry Moore pieces. The gallery may not contain the most important works of these artists but often has interesting exhibitions and allows relaxing meandering. Make sure you stop for some refreshments in the adjoining Caffè delle Arti (see Snack).

Galleria Borghese, Piazzale Scipione Borghese 5, Villa Borghese

Tel: 06 328 10 www.galleriaborghese.it
Open: 9am–7.30pm. Closed Mondays.

The Galleria Borghese set in the gardens of the eponymous park was the first example of a building created specifically to display a private collection of art. The owner of this collection was the Cardinal Scipione Borghese, who commissioned architect Flaminio Ponzio to build his party-pad in 1608. The nephew of Pope Paul V's nephew had a good eye for art

and even picked up some bargain Caravaggio paintings after they had been rejected by other patrons. Sculpture is very well represented in the gallery, and includes important works from masters Canova and Bernini. The former's waxed marble statue of Paolina Borghese (Napoleon's sister) posing as a topless Venus created scandal and notoriety for both artist and patron when it was unveiled. Bernini is the superstar of this collection, whose dramatic works here include the vivid marble depiction of Apollo and Daphne, which bears the sobering inscription 'when we pursue fleeting pleasures we only reap bitter fruits', and the Rape of Proserpina, an erotic tableau of the vituperative god Pluto pressing his crushing hand into the maiden's thigh as he abducts her to his Underworld. The pinacoteca upstairs is groaning with masterpieces, and is a who's who of favourites from the canon of Italian painting from Raphael to Veronese, Rubens to Titian, along with Correggio's semi-pornographic painting of Danaë commissioned for Charles V of Spain. Booking is essential – as far as a week in advance in high season – and visits are timed for every two hours. The good news is the museum is fairly compact and manageable in this time.

Keats/Shelley house, Piazza di Spagna 26, Via Veneto

Tel: 06 678 4235   www.keats-shelley-house.org

Open: 9am–1pm, 3pm–6pm Mon–Fri; 11am–2pm Sun

Among the first Brits to tread the city's streets, the Grand Tour Romantic poets Keats and Shelley have informed much of our conception of Italy, and especially of Rome. This house on the Spanish Steps was a sort of poet hotel, accommodating the likes of Byron, Shelley, Coleridge and Robert Browning on their inspirational passages through the Eternal City. Keats died here of tuberculosis in 1821 and a variety of macabre memorabilia relating to the English Romantic poets is stored here. These include a lock of Keats's hair and his  death mask as well as an urn holding the charred remains of Shelley's skeleton. The comprehensive library contains a melancholia-inducing collection of manuscripts, documents and letters. Keats's apartment above the museum can be rented for weeks or weekends through Britain's Landmark Trust (www.landmarktrust.org.uk).

MACRO, Via Reggio Emilia 54, Villa Borghese

Tel: 06 6710 70400   www.macro.roma.museum

Open: 9am–7pm, public holidays 10am–2pm. Closed Mondays.

Rome's cultural heritage is inevitably bound up in the past – which is why it took quite some time for the city to wake up to the contemporary art scene. Macro (Museo d'Arte Contemporanea Roma) was the first attempt in 1999 to assemble a permanent collection of contemporary art. The collection includes work of Italian artists from the 1960s onwards, including the Arte Povera group, the Scuola di Piazza del Popolo, who took inspiration from the American Pop Art movement, and the Nuova Scuola Romana group, who occupied the former pasta factory, Cerere, in San Lorenzo. The exhibition space is suitably industrial, with steel girders, iron gratings and a somewhat disconcerting glass floor. It was in fact an old brewery. Regular exhibitions of international and Italian artists including Tony Ousler and Marc Quinn draw in an interesting crowd of trendy, urban artophiles. Recently the museum has opened Macro al Mattatoio,

another exhibition space in Testaccio in the old slaughterhouse off Piazza Orazio Giustiniani.

Orto Botanico, Largo Cristina di Svezia, Trastevere
Tel: 06 4991 7106
Open: 9.30am–5.30pm (6.30pm Apr–Oct). Closed Mondays and throughout August.

The Orto Botanico occupies the gardens of the Palazzo Corsini, and was once the property of Queen Cristina of Sweden. Its origins lie in the

medicinal gardens kept by Benedictine monks in the 11th century. The gardens have been the responsibility of La Sapienza University since 1514 and remain an educational resource today. A variety of wild and exotic species make it an enjoyable spot for sunbathing or for simply escaping from the traffic and chaos, and the monumental crumbling staircase and palm trees lend it a sense of faded grandeur.

Palazzo Barberini, Via delle Quattro Fontane 13/via Barberini 18, Via Veneto

Tel: 06 481 4591 www.galleriaborghese.it
Open: 8.30am–7.30pm. Closed Mondays.

This gargantuan baroque palace was commissioned by the Barberini pope Urban VIII and was originally completed in a zealous five years of labour. Sadly there seems to be no one cracking the whip these days, and a seemingly endless restoration process is still under way. This makes viewing erratic and frustrating, and must really irritate the Armed Forces Officers' Club

who share the palazzo with the art gallery. Fortunately the Grand Salone ceiling painting by Pietro da Cortona is permanently on view, depicting the (self-aggrandizing) Allegory of Divine Providence and Barberini Power.

Note the bees, which made up the Barberini coat of arms and appear on buildings all over the city. Cortona's painting is an example of baroque illusionism – he tries to paint away the architecture of the roof to create an unframed vista, like a portal in the sky. The permanent collection is in rotation, and because of the restoration programme it is not possible to guarantee what will be on show. Highlights of the collection include Raphael's *La Fornarina*, Holbein's portrait of *Henry VIII*, Filippo Lippi's *Madonna* and Tintoretto's *Christ and the Woman Taken in Adultery*.

Pantheon, Piazza della Rotonda, Centro Storico
Open: 8.30am–7.30pm Mon–Sat, 9am–6pm Sun; 9am–1pm public holidays

The emperor Hadrian's temple to the Roman deities is the oldest building
in all of Rome, built between AD 119 and 128. The original Pantheon was
even older, built by Marcus Agrippa around 25 BC (but destroyed in a fire in
AD 80), and bears his name on the inscription across the façade.
Consecration as a church in the 7th century saved it from spoil and aban-
donment in the Middle Ages and it's now a mausoleum which contains the
sepulchres of both Raphael and King Victor Emmanuel, the first king of united Italy. Despite suffering many pillages, the Pantheon remains a testament

to the skill and sophistication of Roman architecture. Even the often-critical
Michelangelo proclaimed it to be 'of angelic and not human design'. It's a
shame that these days it has to share a square with too many pigeons and
the golden arches and (greasy odours) of one of Rome's few McDonald's
restaurants. The marble and concrete interior of the building could hold a
giant sphere with a diameter of 43m, and the beguiling 9m hole at the centre of the dome is known as the 'oculus'. This is the only source of light in
the otherwise crepuscular building and is a symbolic link between the temporal and celestial spheres. The Roman concrete used for the dome has
puzzled many. By all accounts an unreinforced dome of these dimensions
could barely hold its own weight, but the Pantheon has stood for centuries.
Bronze beams were taken from the structure by Bernini to melt down into
the baldacchino (altar canopy) for St Peter's in 1628, but the monolithic
bronze doors have stood proud, even if the gold finishing has long since
worn off.

San Clemente, Via San Giovanni Laterano, Via Veneto
Tel: 06 774 0021
Open: 9am (10am Sun)–12.30pm, 3pm–6pm daily

This is the most fantastic archaeological sandwich in all of Rome and the closest you'll get to time travel. The upper church at street level has a theologically complex cycle of mosaics in the apse, created in the 12th century in the Byzantine style. The foliage is a symbol of the living church, which has its roots in the Garden of Paradise, and bears a fruit that is the cross on which Christ was crucified. Christ and the Apostles appear in an allegory of the Lamb of God flanked by a flock of 12 lambs. Near the entrance of the church on the left is a Gothic frescoed chapel depicting the life of St Catherine, which includes the wheel on which she was martyred (thus giving name to the firework). Slip down into the 4th-century basilica church through the door on the right for fading frescoes narrating scenes

from the life of Saint Clement, the fourth pope. Another staircase leads even further back in time to a 2nd-century AD alleyway. On one side is a pagan temple or mithraeum dedicated to the bull-slaying god Mithras, which was a popular cult with the Roman army. On the other side of the old alley are the remains of an early Christian house, or 'titulus', where the first Christians would secretly meet to take Communion before Christianity was legalized in 313. This was no rat hole, however, but one of the few ancient houses with the luxury of running water (still on tap today).

Sant'Ivo alla Sapienza, Corso Rinascimento 40, Centro Storico
Open: 9am–noon, Sundays only

This little-visited and little-known church is a bombastic testament to architect and sculptor Borromini's creativity. The corkscrew spire is a remarkable sight, rising out of the six-point star floor-plan courtyard that merges with the façade in a rhythmic, almost hallucinogenic whirl. Rising along the base of the dome's pillars is the papal Chigi family emblem of the six mountains beneath a star, leaving their stamp of patronage. Unfortunately the church is only open on Sundays, but if you do manage to get inside look for Pietro da Cortona's altarpiece depicting Saint Yves, to whom the church is dedicated. You can, however, see the exterior at anytime from the courtyard (which also doubles up as a dazzling suntrap at lunchtime) off Corso Rinascimento. Look in while you're passing and stop with a slice of pizza – it's well worth the head-spin.

San Luigi dei Francesi, Piazza San Luigi dei Francesi, Centro Storico
Tel: 06 688 271
Open: 8.30am–12.30pm, 3.30–7pm. Closed Thursday afternoons.

This church serves the French community in Rome and is a convenient stop on the way to the Pantheon or Piazza Navona, or indeed after a coffee at

caffeine mecca Sant'Eustachio. The lavish gilded interior verges on the gaudy but it's worth seeing through the bling for the Caravaggio paintings in the crowded chapel on the left. The left-hand panel shows Christ singling out the bewildered Matthew with a shaft of light, Matthew being dragged to his execution is on the right hand panel, while over the altar is an angel telling the bewildered evangelist what to write in his gospel. Caravaggio's chiaroscuro technique can be seen to full brooding effect here. Don't neglect the rest of the church: on the right transept are some Domenichino frescoes from the life of Saint Cecilia.

Santa Maria, Piazza Santa Maria, Trastevere
Tel: 06 581 4802
Open: 7.30am–8pm daily

This church was one of the first Christian basilicas in Rome, possibly even the place where the first Christian mass was celebrated when Christianity was legalized in 313. It sits in a traffic-free cobbled square at the heart of Trastevere where locals congregate around the central fountain and the odd magician or fire-eater entertains tourists. The legend goes that when Christ

was born, a miraculous well of oil sprang from the ground where the church now stands, and flowed down to the Tiber all day. The mosaics on the exterior are from the 13th century and show Mary breastfeeding Christ, surrounded by 10 women with crowns and lanterns on a gold background. Inside is another patchwork of glittering gold mosaics featuring Pietro Cavallini's relaxed Roman-style figures and a Madonna and Child with rainbow overhead. Set into the exterior of the church is a collection of fragments of classical sculpture, medieval tombs and inscriptions, including ancient pagan sarcophagi tablature.

Santa Maria Maggiore, Piazza Santa Maria, Via Veneto
Tel: 06 483 195
Open: 7am–7pm; Museum and tours: 9am–6.30pm

This is one of the earliest of all of Rome's basilicas, dating from the 3rd century. Inside, 5th-century mosaics line the columns above the nave with scenes from the Old Testament. In the apse, Mary appears dressed as a Byzantine empress in a 13th-century mosaic. Rumour has it that the ceiling in the main nave is made from the first shipment of gold from the Americas and a plaque marks the burial-place of Rome's illustrious sculptor Gian

Lorenzo Bernini. Santa Maria Maggiore houses a couple of flamboyantly decorated chapels, including an impostor Sistine Chapel designed by Domenico Fontana for Pope Sixtus V in the late 1500s; bearing no resemblance to the Sistine chapel, it is more a testament to vulgar papal taste than anything else. Every church has a legend, and Santa Maria Maggiore's is one of the more aesthetic. The story goes that in 352 the Virgin Mary appeared to Giovanni the Patrician and told him to build a church on the spot where snow fell the next morning. The miracle is since commemorated every year on 5 August when thousands of flower petals are released from the roof of the church for the Festa della Madonna delle Neve. Tours of the loggia mosaics leave from the baptistery every 10 minutes, relating the details of the legend.

Santa Maria del Popolo, Piazza del Popolo 12, Centro Storico

Tel: 06 361 0836
Open: 7am–noon, 4–7pm Mon–Sat; 8am–7.30pm Sun

Despite the unassuming exterior, this church in the corner of the Piazza del Popolo is in fact a treasure-trove of masterpieces. Raphael mosaics decorate

the cupola of the Chigi chapel. This houses the remains of Agostino Chigi,
the Sienese playboy banker who patronized the arts and partied hard in the

Villa Farnesina. There's an Assumption of the Virgin by Annibale Carracci and
some Pinturicchio frescoes. The real heart-stoppers, however, are the two
unostentatious Caravaggio paintings in the first chapel on the left of the
altar. *The Crucifixion of St Peter* and *The Conversion on the Way to Damascus*
(both from 1600) demand quiet contemplation, and have an emotional,
troubling beauty. The church is apparently haunted by demons, and is said to
be built over the emperor Nero's secret grave.

Santa Maria della Vittoria, Via XX Settembre 17, Via Veneto
Tel: 06 4274 0571
Open: 8.30am–noon, 3.30–6pm. Closed Sunday mornings.

Rather modest by
baroque standards,
this church near the
Via Veneto houses
one of Bernini's most
notorious sculptures,
the sensual *Ecstasy of
St Theresa* (fourth
chapel on the left).
The Spanish mystic
appears floating on a
cloud in a spiritual

trance with a cheeky angel hovering nearby who has just pierced her breast with a burning arrow. Saint Theresa's personal thoughts on her spiritual experience were penned as thus: 'So intense was the pain, I uttered several moans; so great was the sweetness caused by the pain, I never wanted to lose it.' Lucky girl. Sunlight enters through the window above, directing golden rays behind the marble figure and bathing the scene in a glowing light, typical of baroque theatricality. It's enough to make you blush in church.

St Peter's, Piazza di San Pietro, Vatican

Tel: 06 6988 1662 www.vatican.va
Basilica: 7am–6pm (7pm April–September) daily
Dome: 8am–4.45pm (5.45pm May–September) daily

St Peter's Basilica is nothing short of overwhelming and represents the temporal power of the Catholic Church on earth. Some may find the display of wealth and power a little incongruous for an institution expounding the

teachings of Christ, but put this aside for a while and you are left to marvel at one of the most impressive buildings in the world. Inside the hallowed walls are 100 tombs, 91 of which are deceased popes, including the supposed remains of the first ever pope, Saint Peter, whom Christ declared to be the rock on which he would build the church. The much-imitated dome was designed by Michelangelo in 1546; unfortunately he died before its completion. With a diameter of 42.3 metres it is almost as big as the Pantheon, while the church itself can accommodate over 60,000 worshippers. One of the most important, and famous, works in the church is Michelangelo's *Pietà*, an acutely emotional marble sculpture of the Deposition from the Cross, with the dead Christ lying limp in his mother Mary's arms. Unfortunately, since 1972, the sculpture has been kept behind an impenetrable glass screen, when Laszlo Toth, an insane geologist, attacked the work with a hammer. Other precious works include Gina Lorenzo Bernini's bronze baldacchino canopy over the main altar, which apparently is made from bronze beams pillaged from the Pantheon in 1628. Avoid climbing the dome's 320 steps if you are at all claustrophobic, but the vertiginous views over the city are unparalleled. The Sistine Chapel is not in the basilica – you must access it through the Vatican museums, which are a brisk, well-signposted, 15-minute walk away. Dress code is very strict: anyone with shorts, short skirts, bare shoulders or midriffs will be promptly turned away.

Trevi Fountain, Piazza di Trevi, Via Veneto

The Trevi fountain surprises most visitors on first glance because of its unexpectedly cramped quarters. An unbelievably kitsch affair of blowsy sea horses, conch shells, craggy rocks and proud sea gods with their tridents, the fountain has unfortunately descended into a detritus of tacky mass

tourism. Don't even think about recreating Anita Ekberg's famous frolic in the fountain – carabinieri police the square around the clock to deter any wannabe divas. It's best to creep by at night when the square is emptied of its glut of tourists and rose-peddlers, and listen to the pounding of the *aqua vergine*, brought from Emperor Agrippa's 25km aqueduct, on the creamy travertine marble. The sculptor Bernini was originally commissioned to build the fountain, but the patron Pope Urban VII died before he could get started, so it was finally built by Nicolo Salvi for Pope Clement XII in 1762.

Vatican Museums, Viale del Vaticano, Vatican

Tel: 06 6988 3333 www.vatican.va
Open: 8.45–12.20pm (3.20pm weekdays Mar–Oct). Closed Sundays except the last of every month.

Despite the torrential flood of visitors and conditions that would have the EU up in arms if it were for the carriage of livestock, the Vatican museums are a definitive stop on Rome's cultural itinerary and home to the wondrous Sistine Chapel. This immense collection started life with one Greek marble sculpture of Laocoon, which was discovered in a vineyard near Santa Maria Maggiore in 1506. Pope Julius II immediately bought it and put it on

public display a month later. These days most visitors make a beeline for the Sistine Chapel and the prolific work of Michelangelo Buonarotti. He painted the ceiling between 1508 and 1512 and then painted the Last Judgement, spanning the entire wall behind the altar, between 1535 and 1541. Look for Saint Bartholomew holding his flayed skin, which is commonly believed to be Michelangelo's self-portrait. A good tip is to scoot out of the exit on the right-hand side of the chapel labelled 'authorized tour groups only', which takes you directly along to St Peter's – unless you fancy another stretch of ecclesiastical odds and ends and relentless religious merchandising. Don't neglect the other nooks and crannies around the complex, including the Capella di Niccolo' V frescoed by Fra Angelico. Note that all parts of the museum are subject to erratic viewing times and impromptu closures. The other unmissable masterpieces are the Raphael rooms – the apartments of Pope Julius II frescoed between 1508 and 1520 (Giulio Romano completed the work after Raphael's untimely death.) Unglamorous as practicalities are, sensible shoes are essential for a visit, as is bottled water. People often faint in sultry weather.

Villa Farnesina, Via della Lungara 230, Trastevere
Tel: 06 6802 7268   www.lincei.it
Open: 9am–1pm (4pm mid-Mar–June, mid-Sept–Oct; Dec: Mon, Sat). Closed Sundays except the first in the month.

This villa was originally the holiday home for Renaissance playboy banker Agostino Chigi, built between 1508 and 1511 by Baldassare Peruzzi. On the ground floor is the Loggia of Psyche, decorated by Raphael. The two large

pictures on the ceiling are ingeniously painted to simulate tapestries stretched across the roof. The first picture shows the gods putting Psyche though various tests and the second depicts the banquet she held to celebrate her acceptance into the circle of Immortals. This is not Raphael's best work, probably because he was too concerned with wooing Margherita Luti, the baker's daughter (whose portrait, *La Fornarina*, appears in the Palazzo Barberini), and he left the painting to his friends and followers. The master redeems himself, however, with the Loggia of Galatea, who rides her seashell chariot across the waves pulled by dolphins. All lines in the painting converge to frame Galatea's beautiful face, which is based on a Renaissance conception of 'ideal beauty'. Upstairs is the Salone delle Prospettive decorated by Peruzzi, but most enjoyable is Chigi's bedroom, with its sordid Renaissance nouveau-riche decorations by Il Sodoma (so named because of his sexual habits) depicting the marriage of Alexander the Great and Roxanne. Apparently the banquets thrown here by Chigi were so lavish that the gold plates from which the guests ate were hurled into the Tiber after dinner. What his guests didn't know was that nets were in place to fish out the discarded platters ready for next week's party.

shop...

First things first – Rome is not the shopping odyssey many have come to expect from other Italian cities. It lacks the retail clout of Milan and even lags behind Florence. That's the bad news out of the way, now for the good. You're in Italy, where fashion is worshipped, and the Romans turn themselves out with the same national sartorial pride. Women pay special attention to make-up and accessories, which means that there's more choice, and cosmetics and perfume are cheaper.

For the gents, shopping is a more credible leisure activity than in the UK, so seek out the slinky boutiques and unusual labels (especially for shoes and sneakers) rather than plumping for another 'Italian designed' suit. The high-end designer boutiques are all here, from Gucci and Armani to Prada and Chanel. Prices are a little cheaper, but don't expect to be blown away by the variety.

Romans are fairly provincial in their tastes and seem to wear the same styles each season in a limited palette of colours. Dedicated followers of fashion will head for the more niche boutiques, which are sprinkled around the Centro Storico, often off the beaten track, and offer exciting, exclusive labels; however, they can be fiendishly difficult to find – Nuyorica, for example, is hidden away behind the Campo dei Fiori. Others to seek out are Degli Effeti, round the corner from the Pantheon, and Alternative in the Jewish Ghetto. Forays here are far more worthwhile than a trawl along the main shopping streets.

Rome's old-fashioned *profumerie* should not be neglected. These are literally 'perfume shops' but more often than not they are stuffed to the gills with make-up, and all manner of sparkly accessories that are enough to make a magpie weak at the knees.

Italian leather is renowned worldwide and despite the often conservative Italian taste when it comes to clothes, quirkier and more original gloves, bags and shoes are easy to find.

Other national sartorial fascinations include underwear and sunglasses. The Intimissimi chain is as ubiquitous as Starbucks in London and specializes in fun and flirty underwear at rock-bottom prices with stock that changes by the fortnight. As the weather in this part of the Mediterranean is oh-so-clement, swimwear is also of utmost importance.

The Italian obsession with sunglasses (do not even think about taking your sunglasses off between March and November) means that *foto ottica* are hard to miss and prices are generally pretty reasonable, even for designer frames. One of the best and oldest is shops is Ottica Lucchesi on Via del Corso.

Vintage fans should head to Via del Governo Vecchio, a blissful pedestrianized strip lined with some more avant-garde boutiques and quality second-hand

clothes shops, with plenty of spots to tempt you to stop and linger over a cappuccino or *aperitivo*. Antiques and curiosities can be found on the picturesque Via dei Coronari, decorative home furnishings on the lovely ivy-clad Via Giulia and *objets d'art* on Via Margutta. For food lovers a trip to Volpetti delicatessen in Testaccio (see Snack) is an essential pilgrimage if you're after unusual ingredients, pastas and produce – as well as all the ham and cheese you can shake a stick at.

Shopping in Rome (along with dining) in August can be rather futile as many stores close for the long summer holiday. Public holidays are also a write-off for shopping, so consider this when planning your trip.

VIA DEL BABUINO

West of the Spanish Steps the Via del Babuino stretches down to Piazza del Popolo and is a little calmer than the scrum for designer labels on Via dei Condotti. Head here for Missoni, Tiffany's, Costume National and some choice shoe shops. At the bottom is Tad, Rome's only concept store, channelling Colette in Paris and 10 Corso Como in Milan. Here you can pick up all the essentials for a fashionable lifestyle, with stock ranging from Chloe handbags, Marc Jacobs shoes and Seven jeans to CDs, flowers, international magazines and small label perfumes. Across the road the Gente store draws a similar clientele of glamourpusses, hell bent on securing an outfit for the hottest it-crowd opening in town. Thank goodness the Hotel de Russie is at the end of the shopping promenade for a restorative cocktail in the secret garden courtyard.

Armani Jeans Italian designer denim chic. This store is bursting at the seams with the classic jean in all shapes and sizes. A selection of books and magazines provides shoppers with aspirational images from an Armani world.

Aspesi Men's and women's contemporary styles, ranging from sporty to formal, from this modern Milanese label. The conceptual space/shop doubles up as a contemporary art gallery.

Chanel Chic, unequivocal luxury in a cloud of No. 5 perfume, black-and-white classics, with the full make-up range and impeccable, old-fashioned service.

Costume National Purveyors of intellectual chic from the southern Italian label.

Etro Fun, patterned and sparkly men's and women's wear with a slight 1970s retro leaning.

Fabrizio Bulckaen Fashion directional ladies' shoes in original designs and high-quality leather.

Gente Supermodel magnet specializing in hip names from Helmut Lang, Miu Miu, Dsquared and Diane von Furstenberg.

Iceberg Bold women's wear and accessories in vivid colours and patterns. Definitely not for wallflowers.

MAC A bright, bold store with loud music and the full range of US brand cosmetics.

Maria di Ripabianca Luxurious cashmere separates in traditional styles from a family-run business.

Missoni Rainbow-coloured knitwear in dizzying patterns with bikinis, shoes and ties.

Prada Sport Techno fabrics and the ubiquitous red label on discreet, understated pieces that are more suited to *passeggiata*-posing than sweating it out in the gym.

Sergio Rossi Quite simply shoe heaven, with a mouthwatering selection of sexy footwear to put some va-va-voom in your step.

Tiffany Classic luxury jewellery, diamonds and pearls.

Valentino Classic Roman fashion for men and women with signature luxuriant evening wear.

VIA DEI CONDOTTI

Rome's answer to Bond Street, Via dei Condotti joins Via del Corso to the Spanish Steps. The adjoining streets – Via Frattina, Via Borgognona and Via del Babuino – are lined with luxury retail temples. Expect hallowed spaces with haughty assistants and supercilious doormen, but remember that it's your credit card they're after. When the crowds get too much, escape into the nearby Villa Borghese to cool off.

Alberta Ferretti Ethereal, delicate and decidedly feminine women's wear in wispy fabrics and muted colours.

Bruno Magli Classic and sporty shoe designs for men and women with the occasional sparkling party piece alongside briefcases and handbags.

Bulgari *Über-luxe* Italian-designed gems and jewellery.

Burberry Prorsum From classic trench to checked classics, with fashion forward separates mixed in.

Dior Three floors of eye-catching, paparazzi-posing dresses, bags, shoes and jewellery.

Dolce e Gabbana Slick, sensuous, traffic-stopping, lean tailoring and bombastic sexy showstoppers.

Furla Unobtrusive, classic handbags and leather accessories in an ever-rotating selection of styles.

Gucci Rome's flagship store is filled to the rafters with luxury items from the giant of Italian design, all emblazoned with the ubiquitous 'G'.

Hermes Once a French saddler's workshop, now a fashionista hotspot for iconic bags, luxury wear and accessories for men and women.

La Perla Decadent, flirty and often slightly naughty underwear for the ultimate in lingerie indulgence, even if no one else sees it.

Louis Vuitton The original luggage and handbag designs from the much ripped-off label, alongside more recent lines and clothes and shoes from Marc Jacobs.

Marisa Padovan A cornucopia of sultry swimwear for all sizes, from matronly to lapdancer.

Max&Co Younger, sportier and more affordable diffusion line from MaxMara.

Prada Miuccia Prada's reinventions of contemporary classic cool in lingerie, ready-to-wear, sunglasses, shoes and prints for a steady stable of devotees.

Salvatore Ferragamo Classic designs from a shoe-maker who started out as a Neapolitan cobbler and ended up servicing Hollywood stars with luxurious footwear. Understated jackets, coats and accessory line also.

VIA DEL CORSO

Brash and touristy, Via del Corso is the main retail artery splicing the Centro Storico in two from Piazza del Popolo to Piazza Venezia. The majority of shops here are cheap and cheerful, with some choice European high-street favourites such as Zara. The turn-of-the-century shopping mall Galleria Alberto Sordi, with its Art Deco glass-topped roof, reopened in 2003. Inside you'll find the four-storey bookshop Feltrinelli, CK jeans, Trussardi, Guess, AVC and Zara. The Rinascente department store is worth a stop for essentials, although it has a mediocre selection of men's and women's fashions. The jewellery, make-up and accessories on the ground floor are more promising, but for the cosmetics mecca head to La Gardenia at the Piazza Venezia end. Just off Via del Corso, halfway up is the pretty Piazza San Lorenzo in Lucina, home to the beautiful Bottega Veneta store, in a building that used to be part of a 17th-century convent. The gorgeous Ciampini café is opposite for refreshments and a restorative *gelato*.

Diesel Jeanswear, cute accessories and youthful, clubby garments from the harbinger of Italian denim.

Guess Sexy, Mid-West America meets Euro chic in a vast selection of 1980s–inspired jeans and funky, cute accessories.

Intimissimi As ubiquitous in Italy as is Starbucks elsewhere, this enormously popular, affordable underwear store specializes in flirty styles that change by the fortnight.

Miss Sixty Vibrant and young clubby designs in a range of fabrics for those with an individual sense of style, in a psychedelic, '60s-inspired store.

Puma Store This concept store from sponsors of the Italian football team is perennially flooded with shoppers snapping up sneakers, street sportswear and those covetable Stella McCartney designs.

Sisley Benetton's trendy sister-store stocks casual essentials at affordable prices with the occasional, especially delectable shoe or bag.

T'Store An offshoot of the Trussardi empire specializing in bright and breezy nautical, clean-cut, classic T-shirts, jeans and shoes.

VIA FRATTINA

Angelo di Nepi African- and Eastern-inspired brightly coloured designs in linen, silk and taffeta from this home-grown Roman designer.

AVC by Adriana V. Campanile Extremely successful shoe boutique with everything from stilettos to ballet pumps at discreet prices, with a capsule collection of clothing to boot.

Demoiselle Stunning swimwear to make even the steeliest lifeguard blush, from labels Pucci, Pin-Up, Delfina, Missoni and La Perla.

Hugo Boss One for the boys, with conventional, well-made, classic suits alongside more casual and sporty lines, and all the essentials from aftershave to socks and underwear.

Laltramoda Seasonal catwalk-inspired collections with basic knits in cashmere and cotton, and desirable coats and suits.

Patrizia Pepe Florentine glamour comes to Rome with contemporary styles and sexy, feminine shapes.

Versace Jeans Couture High-octane, sexy styles in a rainbow palette of colours for men and women, with leather jackets, sunglasses and shoes.

VIA BORGOGNONA

Calvin Klein Minimalist American chic on three floors with casual, chic and formal wear for men and women upstairs and the eponymous watches, jewellery and sunglass range on the ground floor.

Fratelli Rosetti Classic brogues, loafers and golfing shoes for men with a sprinkling of more modern styles for both sexes.

Galassia Cutting-edge, avant-garde chic with international labels, from Vivienne Westwood and Ann Demeulemeester to Jean Paul Gaultier and Marc Jacobs shoes.

Hogan The eponymous bowling shoes and leather sneakers and handbags in a vast array of colours.

Laura Biagiotti The Roman 'queen' of cashmere in a boutique that was once a theatre.

Moschino An exuberantly designed and decorated store with fun and frivolous fashion dashed with an accent of wit.

Roberto Cavalli has assumed the same connotations in Italy as the Burberry check with footballers' wives in the UK, but the 'jungle chic' and flashy styles have their own unique appeal.

VIA DEL GOVERNO VECCHIO

This is one of Rome's most gorgeous streets – removed from the tourist fray but still convincingly central since it's just behind the Piazza Navona. It was once lined with artisans and craftsmen, but these have given way over time to small independent boutiques, wine bars and cafés. This is also where you're likely to find the highest concentration of vintage and second-hand clothing shops. The Romans have yet to fully develop the passion for thrift, which means that all the good stuff isn't immediately snapped up, and with a bit of shopping serendipity you may just chance upon that pair of once-in-a-lifetime never-been-worn Pollini boots.

Abiti Usati An atmospheric cornucopia of second-hand jeans, retro cashmere, biker jackets and vintage designer labels.

Arsenale Niche items for avant-garde dressers, including extravagant evening wear in a Manhattan loft-style space.

Josephine de Huertas A favourite with the it-crowd, this French designer's boutique stocks an eclectic mix of Joseph, Diane von Furstenberg and Paul Smith.

Luna & L'Altra Intelligentsia chic with Issey Miyake, Dries van Noten and Gaultier in this intimate boutique situated in a 17th-century *palazzo*.

Maga Morgana Quirky and ultra-feminine designs with whimsical details.

Omero e Cecilia Sixties lovechildren Omero and Cecilia run this fabulous emporium of vintage finds, from Burberry macs to 1950s sundresses and a stunning selection of original second-hand shoes and boots at reasonable prices.

Vestiti Usati Cinzia Only the very best of vintage street style makes it onto the racks of Cinzia Fabbri's stylish boutique.

MONTI

244 Panisperna Via An eclectic boutique in a former art gallery, where creativity is still reflected in an eccentric collection of shoes (including Robert Clergerie) and an avant-garde line in clothing.

Archivia *Via del Boschetto* Funky homeware and furnishings, from rose print plates to comfortable classic bedlinen.

De Grillis *Via di Campo Carleo*, 26 Sexy designer styles from each season, including Missoni knit dresses, YSL sandals, Alessandro dell'Aqua and Alexander McQueen, tucked away behind the ruins of the Emperor Trajan's markets.

LOL *Piazza degli Zingari 11* A shop that doubles up as an exhibition space, with classy cashmere separates, accessories and luxury homeware.

Tina Sondergaard *Via del Boschetto* Dressmaker Tina uses retro and vintage fabrics to make original and sexy creations that include tea-dresses, coats and skirts.

CAMPO DEI FIORI AND AROUND

Loco *Via dei Baullari* Weird and wonderful shoe designs and glamorous sneakers, popular with fashionistas and footwear-worshipping Italians.

Nuyorica *Piazza Pollarola* The definitive stop for the city's hottest shoes, handbags, accessories and small label international designers, from Lara Bohinc jewellery to Chloe swimsuits and Balenciaga bags.

Only Hearts *Piazza della Chiesa Nuova* Romantic underwear and lacy, luxuriant garments to lounge in, from Manhattan purveyors of delicate underwear as outerwear.

PANTHEON

Degli Effeti *Piazza Capranica* Three branches of the pioneering Roman fashion store are situated in the same square behind the Pantheon, with exclusive labels from Comme des Garcons, Y2, J Watanabe, Yamamoto and Martin Margiela. Great sneakers in the men's branch.

VIA COLA DI RIENZO

Via Cola di Rienzo stretches from Piazza Risorgimento by the Vatican to Ponte Margherita and Piazza del Popolo in the centre of town. This civilized shopping parade is dominated by the well-heeled Prati set, with their rinses and preened pooches. Food is a big attraction here because of the Castroni delicatessen (and Franchi next door, see Snack), where ex-pats stock up on all and sundry international gourmet products.

Benetton Classic essentials from the high-profile, perennial Italian high-street store.
Coin Department store. Better for accessories than fashion, but with a very highly recommended cosmetics and beauty department.
La Cicogna Upmarket own-label classic children's and maternity wear, plus tiny versions of designer ranges.
Laltramoda A second branch of the Roman boutique stocking flattering and sexy catwalk-inspired women's wear.
Mango Two floors of Spanish high-street favourite with a bevy of seasonal trends to choose from.
Sabon A branch of the NYC store selling delicious hand-made scented scrubs, creams and soaps with aromatherapy oils.

ELSEWHERE

Alternative *Piazza Mattei*
Alternative, as the name suggests, is off the beaten track, behind Piazza Venezia in the cobbled heart of the Jewish Ghetto. Gunmetal grey walls and glitzy chandeliers show off slinky garments from Alessandro dell'Aqua, Michael Kors, Hussein Chalayan and Missoni's desirable diffusion range. Once you've scratched your sartorial itch, have a drink in Bar Taruga next door, a decidedly kitsch yet chic affair named after the 'turtle' fountain in the same square.

MARKETS

Porta Portese Piazza di Porta Portese

Open: 7am–1pm Sundays

The Porta Portese flea market is based around the Piazza di Porta Portese but in reality sprawls through deepest Trastevere and the brinks of Testaccio every Sunday. It may have become something of a tourist magnet but if you can handle the scrum and the early start (get there by 9am at the latest), in among the cut-price electrical goods and football shirts there are occasional gems to be found, especially around the Piazza Ippolito Nievo. Prices are cheap but be prepared to haggle for that cashmere sweater and 1920s Russian clock.

Via Sannio

Open: 8.30am–1.30pm Mon–Fri; 8.30am–6pm Sat

San Giovanni lies behind the city gates by the cathedral of San Giovanni in Laterano. It may be a little scruffy but rewards are there for *pochi soldi* for those prepared to sift through the heap of stock. Some stalls are more organized, displaying their garments on hangers, and there are some nice vintage 1970s dresses up for grabs, but the majority build anthills on tables and these require some dedicated rummaging. Finds may include Burberry macs and vintage silk negligees.

La Sofitta Sotto I Portici, Piazza Augusto Imperatore

Open: 9am–7pm, 1st and 3rd Sunday of the month

A gem of an antiques market, just next to the outsize birdbath that is the mausoleum of Augustus. Stalls are heaped together in the colonnades of an old Fascist state building and are conveniently placed for a spot of browsing before or after Sunday brunch at Gusto' in the same square. Anything from vintage World War I flying hats to turn-of-the-century kaleidoscopes can be picked up for a song, or indeed a dance – the same space is given over to tango dancers on certain days.

OUTLET SHOPS

Rome's fashion outlets are just outside the city and a little tricky to reach without a car. The best is the mock Ancient Rome outlet 'village' 15km past the EUR suburbs in the Castelli Romani. Over 90 stores groan with a bevy of designer-label stock ranging from CK Jeans and Dolce & Gabbana to Tommy Hilfiger, Diesel and Etro, with reductions from 30% to 70%.

Castel Romano Outlet Via Ponte di Piscina Cupa 64, Castel Romano
Tel: 06 505 0050 www.mcarthurglen.it Open: 10am–9pm daily

play...

They've always been a lazy lot, those Romans – so when it comes to sports, spectating is what they're generally best at. The most religious following is for football, and after the nation's 2006 World Cup victory, passions are ever more ardent.

The city is ferociously divided between supporters of AS Roma (red and yellow strip) and SS Lazio (blue and white) and any chat struck up in bars over the (decidedly un-masculine) pink newspaper *Gazzetta dello Sport* will revolve around the question '*Di che squadra sei?*', or 'Which do you support?' If you're asked, it's probably advisable to declare allegiance with AS Roma, as the Lazio team are notorious for their alleged right-wing and racist sympathies.

There's no shortage of glamorous tournaments during the season to bring the jet-set out in force. Come late spring the pop of *prosecco* corks resounds at the Tennis Open in May and at the show-jumping event in the Villa Borghese.

But for those keen to practise their grip or their backhand, choices are a little limited, and Italians tend to keep their luxury sports clubs rather exclusive. Furthermore, the way Romans see it, it's better to spend your time gorging on

top-notch cuisine rather than sweating it out under the sun. This means that the '*deliciaie vitae*' of food and wine are well catered for with courses in connoisseurship.

In Italy the beach is treated with an

almost religious reverence, and Rome's proximity to the coast means that many Romani flee at the weekend from the sweaty clutches of the city for fresh air, water sports and staying supine in the sun. The little-known strip of coastline between Rome and Naples warrants exploration, from the sand dunes of Sabaudia to the golden beaches and Mediterranean loveliness of Circeo San Felice, Gaeta and Sperlonga.

More unusual activities, such as hot-air ballooning or nocturnal horse-riding excursions under the stars on the ancient Appian Way, will delight those who are seeking a more adventurous or romantic way to experience Rome.

Romani just love a festival (no doubt a throwback to days of 'bread and circuses') and mayor Walter Veltroni has proved to be a very enthusiastic patron of the arts, rallying support for all number of festivals to promote Rome's cultural identity in the 21st century. The Estate Romana festival ignites the city with a feast of cultural happenings during the summer months, and the International Photography Festival has proved to be a serious player on the international art scene.

Aware of the civilizing effect of baths and spas since ancient times, Rome has taken inspiration from its Eastern neighbours with the arrival of some truly sybaritic spas and Turkish baths. Influences from the East extend to holistic yoga and massage centres to calm your cockles in what can be an exhausting and chaotic metropolis.

Rome comes into its own when in the throes of a festival or city-wide celebration, and never more so than during the Estate Romana's 3-4 month festival, with literary, dance, theatre music and art events in every pocket of the city (www.estateromana.it). From April the Fotografia Festival Internazionale di Roma (International Photography Festival) is held, with exhibitions and talks in a variety of locations around town (www.fotografiafestival.it). Then in September Enzimi, the most progressive and experimental in contemporary culture, is showcased around Piazza Vittorio and Termini (www.enzimi.festivalroma.org).

FOOD AND WINE COURSES

Città del Gusto, Via Enrico Fermi 161, Ostiense
Tel: 06 551 1221   www.gamberorosso.it

The vast, six-storey restructured warehouse is Rome's contemporary palace to food and wine, courtesy of the Gambero Rosso culinary publishing and media giant. The 5,000sq.m complex in Ostiense includes a wine bar, restaurant, shop and TV studios, and offers various courses in food and wine all year round.

Il Palazzetto International Wine Academy, Vicolo del Bottino 8, Via Veneto
Tel: 06 699 0878   www.wineacademyroma.com

The International Wine Academy occupies a 16th-century *palazzo* by the Spanish Steps, and offers prestigious courses ranging from half-day and evening classes to masterclasses with leading figures from the world of wine. It also organizes small group tours to local wine regions and vineyards.

FOOTBALL

A national sporting institution, football beats in the life-blood of most Italians, and has the power to reduce grown men to tears. There are three Roman football teams: AS Roma, SS Lazio (both in Serie A) and the little-known Serie C Lodigliani team. The two main teams are vehement rivals for a hotbed of 'romanisti' (red and yellow) activity, head south to Testaccio. Both sides come into battle during the electrifying Rome Derby matches, which take place at the Stadio Olimpico. Hardcore 'Laziali' (blue and white) sit in the Curva Nord. The 82,000-seater stadium was rebuilt for the 1960 Rome Olympics and then expanded for the 1990 World Cup.

For a calendar of the season's Serie A football matches, go to www.serieacalcio.com.

Stadio Olimpico, Via Foro Italico, Foro Italico
Tel: 06 36 851

GOLF

Golf is a rather exclusive sport in Rome, and most clubs will require proof of membership and handicap.

Circolo del Golf Roma Aquasanta, Via Appia Nuova 716, Appia Nuova
Tel: 06 780 3407   www.golfroma.it
Open: 8am–sunset. Closed Mondays.

Claims to be Italy's first ever golf club and boasts a dramatic setting framed by the walls of an ancient aqueduct and with views of the dome of St Peter's.

HELICOPTER RIDES

Take a tour in a helicopter, with 60 minutes costing €3,000 for a six-pax helicopter, or transfer from Rome to Capri, Monte Carlo and Costa Smeralda in Sardegna. The same company offers an air tour of Rome for €80 per person, departing from Rome Urbe airport. They also hire out scooters, bikes and cars.

Eco Move Rent, Via Varese 48–50, Termini
Tel: 06 4470 4518   www.ecomoverent.com

Cavalieri dell'Appia Antica, Via dei Cerceni 15, Appia Antica
Tel: 06 780 1214

Open: 10am–6pm. Closed Mondays and two weeks in August.

This company organizes atmospheric and tranquil excursions on horseback down the Appian Way, Rome's oldest road, which reaches down into the south of the peninsula. Now it's overgrown in parts, with the mosses of time even more evocative of past centuries during moonlight rides. €20 for an hour's ride.

If you want to watch horse-riding rather than participate, then join the jet-set, who descend on Villa Borghese between late April and early May to witness the annual *prosecco*-fuelled showjumping event, Il Concorso Ippico Internazionale di Piazze di Siena. Information at www.piazzadisiena.com.

Aerophile 5500, Galoppatoio, Villa Borghese
Tel: 06 3211 1511   www.aerophile.it

Open: 9.30am–sunset. Closed in winter.   €15

For an alternative, vertiginous view of the city, the world's largest tethered hot air balloon rises daily above the Villa Borghese from the top of Via Veneto in Via del Galoppatoio. The balloon floats some 500 feet above ground level, inviting claims that it is the 'eighth hill' of Rome, and provides spectacular views of the city.

Despite being somewhat eclipsed by football fever, rugby enjoys a certain status in the *bel paese*. The national team takes part in the Six Nations championship and plays home matches at the Stadio Flaminio. Indigenous Roman team RDS Roma play at Stadio Tre Fontane, where tickets are a mere €5.

Stadio Flaminio, Viale Tiziano, Flaminio
Tel: 06 3685 7309   www.federugby.it

Stadio Tre Fontane, Via delle Tre Fontane, EUR
Tel: 06 592 2485

SAILING

Such proximity to the Lazian coast means that come early summer most
Romani head for the sea each weekend for a spot of sunbathing and sailing.
San Felice Circeo is an Arcadian spot along the coast, perfect for water
sports and virtually tourist-free. The yacht club here offers five-day sailing
courses throughout the summer months with English speaking instructors,
and has an active calendar of sailing activities and regattas.
Circolo Yacht Vela Club, Via Ammiraglio Bergamini 140, San Felice Circeo
www.cycv.it

SCOOTERS, BIKES AND MOTORBIKES

Do as the Romans do and scoot about town on a '*motorino*' or 'scooter'. It's
by far the most convenient way of traversing the city and seeing things off
the beaten track. Remember that the wearing of helmets at all times is one
of the few rigorously enforced laws. Bicycles are another option for the
brave – the traffic-cloggedRoman streets may be more than what you're
used to and cycling on the cobbles can be a real bone-rattler, but there are
a couple of cycle lanes along the banks of the Tiber, and it makes for speedy
sightseeing. If you just fancy a spin for the afternoon, visit the Villa Borghese,
which has plenty of bike rental stands, including tandems and the popular
buggy bikes for four to six people.

Bici e Baci, Via del Viminale 5, Centro Storico
Tel: 06 482 8443
Open: 8am–7pm daily

Has bikes and scooters for hire, and also organizes guided tours on vintage
motorbikes.

Cyclo', Via Cavour 80, Centro Storico
Tel: 06 481 5669

Will deliver scooters to any address in Rome for €10.

Due Ruote Rent, Via Farini 3, Villa Borghese
Tel: 06 481 8185
Open: 24 hours daily

SPAS AND BEAUTY

Acanto, Piazza Rondanini 30, Centro Storico
Tel: 06 6813 6602 www.acantobenessere.it
Open: 10am–8pm. Closed Sundays.

Acanto is behind the Pantheon and adjoins the Caffè Universale. Inside it is like a Roman spa of old, with exposed brickwork, classical arches, the soothing sounds of running water and luxuriant treatments fit for an emperor. This is contrasted with futuristic lighting and 21st-century treatments (such as floating colour therapy). Aside from the exquisitely sumptuous *hammam*, there are areas for manicures and pedicures, reflexology and facials, and a relaxation zone to bliss out with a herbal tea post-treatment. For €400 couples can enjoy a Turkish bath strewn with rose petals, a cocktail and 90-minute massage each. Sheer romantic indulgence.

Baan Thai, Borgo Angelico 22a, Prati
Tel: 06 6880 9459 www.baanthai.it
Open: 11am–10pm daily

In the shadow of the Vatican, this traditional Thai house offers a soothing Eastern antidote to Western chaos through relaxing and invigorating massage. Treatments range from the classic Thai massage (involving fairly physical manipulation) to deep-tissue massages with oils and ayurvedic techniques. Things are rounded off with a jasmine tea and some Turkish delight to prepare you for the next gruelling round of sightseeing. The late opening hours make it a great place to stop at the end of a long day.

Centro Olistico Day Spa (CODS), Piazza Pollarola 31, Centro Storico

Tel: 06 6819 2347

Open: 10am–8pm. Closed Sundays and Mondays.

The atmosphere in this city centre 'day spa' is more clubby beauty salon than oasis of tranquillity, but it does boast a quick 'in and out' Turkish *hammam*. All the usual waxing, facials, massage and nail technology are on offer, plus they seem to have a special enthusiasm for tanning. There are even sun beds with built-in LCD displays so you can tap your toes to MTV hits while you bronze. Next door is essential shoe-stop – Manhattan-style – NuYorica, so either prep your feet with a luxury pedicure pre-shopping or chill out with a massage in here after a pulse-racing spree.

Elleffe, Via di San Calisto 6, Trastevere

Tel: 06 5833 3875

Open: 10am–8pm. Closed Sundays and Mondays.

Sometimes Italians really do do it better, especially when it comes to hairdressing. With such steadfast ideas about beauty coursing through their aesthetic veins it's unlikely an Italian hairdresser will make you look anything less than as fabulous as you can be. This cool little boutique salon is dappled with graffiti from the outside and decorated with contemporary paintings inside, and English-speaking staff will work just as many wonders for contemporary glamourpusses on holiday as they do for their usual dedicated Roman fashion set. Not a blue rinse or Marcel wave in sight.

Nailbar, Via Giulia 72, Centro Storico

Tel: 06 683 8911   www.gamax.it

Open: 10am–8pm. Closed Sunday and Monday's.

For those annoying moments when you break a nail or need your acrylics filled or fresh silk wraps, help is at hand at the Nailbar on the peaceful and lovely Via Giulia. This salon is more of a gallery than the kind of nail bar on the UK high street, specializing in 'concept design' for hands and nails.

El Spa, Via Plinio 15c/d, Prati

Tel: 06 6819 2869 www.elspa.it

Traditional Turkish baths in upmarket Prati with a host of ayurvedic treatments and massages, from hot stones and crystals to shiatsu, stone therapy
and lymphatic drainage. The lantern-lit baths are rapturously romantic and
have ceilings perforated with tiny lights resembling stars.

SWIMMING

For Olympic-size open-air public pools head to the suburbs, either in EUR
or off the Appian Way. If you stick in the centre be prepared to pay for the
privilege, especially if you go to a hotel pool to swim. If you just want to
laze and lounge over a few cocktails head up to the Radisson SAS rooftop,
which is free.

Oasi della Pace, Via degli Eugenii 2, Castelli Romani

Tel: 06 718 4550

Open: 9am–6.30pm, mid-June–end of September

A rather bucolic choice set among hedges and cypress trees.

Parco dei Principi, Via Frescobaldi 5, Villa Borghese

www.parcodeiprincipi.com

Open: 10am–6.30pm May–September

On the edge of Villa Borghese gardens in the grounds of the five-star hotel -
will cost €50 for the day.

Piscina delle Rose, Viale America 20, Viale Europa

Tel: 06 592 6717 www.piscinadellerose.it

Open: 9am–7pm (10pm July–August) May–September

TENNIS

Every year in May the Italian Open (Masters Series) tournament comes to Rome. Tennis stars play on clay courts at the Foro Italico park near the Stadium. For the rest of us, the Circolo della Stampa has clay and synthetic grass courts and is owned by the Italian Journalists Association.

Circolo della Stampa, Piazza Mancini 19, Flaminio
Open: daily, 9am–10pm (8pm Sat–Sun)

Foro Italico Tennis Stadium, Viale dei Gladiatori 31, Foro Italico
www.federtennis.it

YOGA

L'Albero e la Mano, Via della Pelliccia 3, Trastevere
Tel: 06 581 2871 www.lalberoelamano.it
Open: times. Closed Sundays and mid-July–mid-September.

Ashtanga and Hatha yoga as well as bellydancing, t'ai chi, shiatsu, and ayurvedic and Thai massage, off a pretty cobbled side street in Trastevere.

Bikram Yoga, Via Aurelia 190, Prati
Tel: 06 4549 2898 www.bikramyogaroma.it

The craze for 'sweaty yoga' has reached Rome. There's a centre just beyond the Vatican walls for devotees of this high-intensity, high-temperature practice. Classes are in Italian and English.

EMERGENCY NUMBERS

Ambulance (special number for tourists) 06 422 371

Police 112

Fire Service 115

In medical emergencies head to one of the '*pronto soccorso*' accident and emergency departments. These are located on the Isola Tiberina (Ospedale Fatebenefratelli) and the Circonvallazione Gianicolense, 87 (Ospedale San Camillo).

MONEY

Italy invented banking, and there is no shortage of ATMs or what are known as '*bancomats*'. Bank opening hours are notoriously erratic, generally from around 8.30am till lunchtime and then again – for anything from 2 hours to 45 minutes – from 3.30pm or 4pm. Bureaus de change are dotted around the Centro Storico, especially on Via del Corso. Bring a passport when making purchases by credit card.

PHARMACIES

'*Farmacie*' are identified by a green cross and normal opening hours are 8.30am–1pm and 4–8pm Mon–Sat. There is a 24-hour pharmacy at Termini station (Piazza del Cinquecento 49–51, tel: 06 488 0019). Pharmacies also offer advice for minor medical complaints and sell antibiotics without the need for a prescription, as well as emergency contraception – but be prepared for raised eyebrows if you're within earshot of the Vatican.

PUBLIC TRANSPORT

Due to the hegemony of underground archaeological remains, the metro system in Rome is rather limited, with only two lines servicing a paltry number of areas. Lines A and B cross only once at Termini station. A third line, 'C', is in progress, which means that Line A shuts down daily at 9pm. Line B runs daily until 11.30pm, and 12.30am on Saturdays. Tickets cost €1 and can be bought from machines inside stations or at news kiosks and tobacconists. Each ticket is valid for 75 minutes and is also valid on Rome's bus and tram network, which means that in the space of 75 minutes you may catch a metro, bus and tram as long as you validate your ticket on each leg. Yellow stamping machines can be found near the front and back of buses and trams. Joyride at your peril. Fines are steep and inspectors unsympathetic to clueless foreigners.

SMOKING

Since January 2005 it has been illegal to smoke indoors in public places in Rome.

TAXIS

Hailing a taxi in the street can be frustratingly futile as Roman cabs park at ranks, designated by a blue sign, which reads TAXI in white. In the Centro Storico there are ranks at Largo Argentina, Pantheon, Piazza Venezia and by the Spanish Steps. If you're in the city centre make sure the tariff is on 1, as opposed to 2, which is the higher tariff for outside the city ring road (if you're heading to the airport, for example). Supplemented charges depend on baggage, number of passengers and whether it is a public holiday or Sunday.

Taxis from the Fiumicino and Ciampino airports into Rome will cost €35–45. Do not take an unlicensed cab from either the airport or Termini station, since you will be extortionately ripped off. Radio taxis can be called on 06 3570.

TELEPHONES

The international dialling code for Italy is +39 and the local code for Rome is 06. When dialling outside Italy the code is +39 06. Phone cards can be bought at *tabacchi*, which have a black sign with a white 'T', or at newsstands.

WATER

Drinking water from the tap in Rome is perfectly safe, while archaic-looking drinking fountains all around the Centro Storico are serviced with the *aqua vergine*, *aqua paola* and *aqua felice* ancient aqueducts, bringing soft, delicious H_2O from the countryside.

Hg2 Rome

index